JN096771

Comparative Culture and Society: A textbook to supplement discussion, debate, presentation, and writing classes

1st Edition

© 2020 Daniel Velasco

ISBN: 978-4-86693-095-4

About this textbook

This textbook contains fifteen short units that give students opportunities to discuss, debate, present, and write about global topics and issues. Most units are paired with one country, so that each topic can be viewed from that cultural perspective, which can then be compared to students' own cultural perspectives and experience. This textbook integrates such fields as intercultural communication, psychology, sociology, and anthropology, as well as elements from the field of English-as-a-Second-Language (ESL) / English-as-a-Foreign-Language (EFL).

In essence, this is a Content and Language Integrated Learning (CLIL) textbook, meaning students learn content while simultaneously developing their English language skills. This does not mean that this textbook is designed exclusively for ESL/EFL students. Actually, many native English speakers can benefit from reviewing appropriate language choices and public speaking skills contained in each unit. In other words, students learn or improve their 1) English skills by using it to communicate in class, 2) critical thinking and communication skills by preparing for discussions, debates, and presentations, and 3) cultural intelligence by studying different cultures and societies, and comparing them to their home country or past experiences abroad.

Most units have the following sections:

- a vocabulary list—This list should ideally be studied before the lesson so that students can use the words and phrases in their discussion, presentations, and papers. There are activities at the end of the textbook (pp. 129-135) that can help students learn them.
- a short reading—This reading is brief enough so that it can be read silently or aloud in class. The latter is recommended, as the benefits of hearing books read aloud include improved comprehension, reduced stress, and expanded exposure to different types of materials (Marchessault & Larwin, 2013). The readings include charts, graphs, and URLs to online videos and other materials that will further enhance the learning and understanding of each topic.
- activities for individuals and small groups—These activities give the students the chance to reflect on the topics and their own cultural experiences, and then share them with a partner or small group. The activities are usually in the reading section.

- discussion questions—There are three discussion questions for each unit, and all the questions are meant to promote critical thinking about topics and themes for more than one cultural group. The goal is to start a class discussion where everyone is sharing their thoughts, opinions, and ideas in an open and respectful manner.
- speaking strategies—Strategies are separated into three categories: general discussion skills, academic presentation skills, and debate skills. Many of the skills learned in these categories can also be applied to regular everyday conversations, as well as academic writing assignments.
- final unit assignments—Every final assignment is designed to help students summarize and add to each unit's content, sharpen their research skills, develop their speaking skills, and enhance their writing or presentation-making skills. While many of the final assignments also serve as springboards for the next unit, students should always try to utilize the knowledge gained from previous units to current ones.

Throughout each unit are URL links to online materials and videos that make learning modern, interactive, and fun (see **Disclaimer** on page 140). Since there are a lot of videos and images to share, the instructor may want to show the content on his or her main classroom screen (using the school's laptop and/or LCD projector, for example), or allow students to use their own devices (if the technology is available) to access and view them together in class. If the latter is used, classroom supervision and management should be a top priority. The main reason for using online videos is that it lowers the cost of the textbook while using an application that everyone is familiar with.

The last point to consider is this: While the units focus on one particular country to illustrate and enhance each theme, students and instructors are not stuck with only talking about that country. The units are meant to be starting points, but the overall goal is always critical thinking about global issues that leads to respectful discussions and deep cultural learning. Some topics can be a little controversial, so it is important to build a good rapport with everyone in order to create a safe place where there is freedom to openly express thoughts and opinions.

The units, their themes, and the countries that are connected to them are listed on the next page. Have fun exploring and comparing culture and society!

Contents   Page

UNIT 1: WHO AM I (AS A CULTURAL BEING)?

Vocabulary List

Check the meaning of the words and phrases below. Then use them in the activities in this unit.

1) culture

2) society

3) race

4) ethnicity

5) gender

6) sexual orientation

7) socioeconomic status

8) identity

9) profession

10) descriptor

Unit Reading and Activities

It is difficult to begin a discussion on culture and society without knowing what culture and society means. It means different things to different people, and the only way to be sure that everyone in this class has a shared understanding of their meanings is to create one together.

Activity Get into small groups (3-4 students in each group), and create one definition for *culture* and *society* that everyone agrees on.

Write your group's final definitions here.

1) For our group, *culture* means...

2) For our group, *society* means...

Think about your definitions for *culture* and *society*, and talk about this question with your group: *What is cultural identity?* Write your group's ideas in the box!

When everyone is finished, share your definitions and ideas with the class!

As you can see, *culture* has many different meanings, so it is likely that the combined definitions of every group create a pretty good working definition for this class! According to the Cambridge English Dictionary (n.d.), *culture* is "the way of life of a particular people, especially as shown in their ordinary behavior and habits, their attitudes toward each other, and their moral and religious beliefs." Culture is made up of a lot of different things, like values, expectations, appropriate behaviors, social expectations, and symbols.

If we know this about culture, then cultural identity can simply be defined as someone who feels like they fit in with or belong to a certain cultural group! It is interesting to note that cultural identity is not static, meaning it can change. If someone moves to a foreign country and stays there for a long period of time, it is possible that he or she will have the ability to identify with more than one culture.

Who am I?

Let's think about all of the aspects of culture and society, and how they help us create our cultural identity. There are so many parts of us that it can be difficult to label! However, we're going to try. Take a look at this chart:

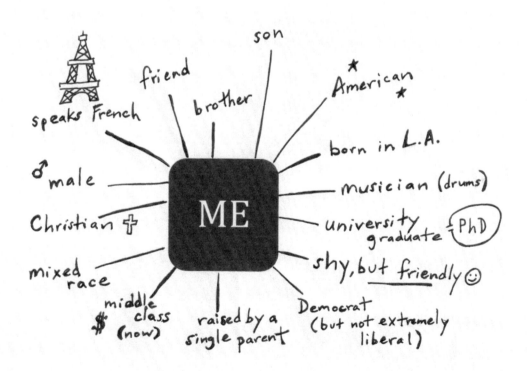

This is an example of a "ME" chart. As you can see, there are many ways that we can "label" or categorize ourselves, and while "brother" may be very different from being a "university graduate," if you think about them carefully, culture plays a big part in both! For example, being a brother means being part of a family, and families are one part of a cultural group (and can also be considered a cultural group itself). Another example is being a "university graduate." Being a graduate means you attended school, and schools are not only institutions in a culture, but they have their own culture, as well! Therefore, schools, like families, can also be considered a cultural group. All of these aspects of ourselves are what make up our *cultural identity*, but there are many more other than what you see in the chart above!

Activity Look at the "ME" box below. Create your own chart like the one on page 7! Try to come up with at least ten different aspects of who you are. Feel free to be creative and add pictures or symbols!

Now that we've defined important terms, and examined what makes up cultural identity, let's dive deeper into cultural identity!

Take a look at the **Cultural Descriptors Worksheet**. For this worksheet, we will be looking at dominant cultural descriptors. In other words, what are some clear, strong parts of your culture that make a person part of that culture? These parts can be seen as both positive and negative, so it is important that we can identify both.

For example, you might write, "only one major ethnic group in my country" (monoethnic). But is this a positive aspect or a negative aspect? Arguments can be made for both, actually!

One way to look at a monoethnic culture is from a collectivist perspective. In a collectivist society, the best interest of the entire community comes first (before an individual), and this is positive because it means people take care of their communities before they take care of themselves. (Note: This is a generalization, of course, and does not apply to every person in these types of cultures). Examples of monoethnic and collectivist countries include Japan, China, and South Korea.

On the other hand, this can also be seen as negative because it means that differences are sometimes frowned upon. For example, there is a saying in Japan: "The nail that sticks out gets hammered down" (出る杭は打たれる). This means that being different from everyone else (or not going along with the group) is bad. Being different has led to bullying in schools and even companies (Asian Correspondent, 2019).

Activity Think about four dominant descriptors in your culture. After you come up with four, think about positive *and* negative sides of each descriptor, and then write your answers in the appropriate sections below. You can do this alone or with a partner/small group!

"Hardworking" can be seen as both a positive and negative cultural descriptor.

Cultural Descriptors Worksheet

Descriptors

Three dominant descriptors in my culture are:

1.

2.

3.

Positives

One positive thing about each descriptor is:

1.

2.

3.

Negatives

One negative thing about each descriptor is:

1.

2.

3.

Discussion Questions

1. Using the "ME" chart, discuss the different aspects of yourself with a partner. How many different parts of your cultural identity did you make? Be sure to explain each point. For example, if you write "Sister," are you the oldest in a big family or an only child? How did this impact your relationships with your family?

2. Exchange your Cultural Descriptor Worksheet with a partner, and use their answers to interview them. The goal is to get them talking about the positive and negative sides of their cultural descriptors. For example, if they wrote, "My culture avoids conflict," then you can ask, "So, can you explain why your culture avoids conflict? Is this mostly good or bad for people who are not from that culture?"

3. Review the vocabulary list with a partner or small group. Take turns explaining each word or phrase, and give an example of each one.

Speaking Strategies: General Speaking Skills, Part I

The first step to becoming a good speaker is not the words you use, but the way you use your body. How you sit or stand, where you look (or don't look), the way you move your hands are all extremely important when speaking to people. Whether it's one person or a roomful of people, all of these parts are important. Let's look at each one, and then apply them to the Speaking Assignment below!

How to stand: Your feet should be shoulder-width apart, and your back should be straight, and not hunched over. Imagine you have a string attached to the top of your head, and someone is pulling it straight up to the ceiling!

Where to look: One big problem with many speakers is maintaining eye contact. Keeping your eyes on one person may feel strange at first, but it shows you are listening and interested in what they are saying. With more than one person, focus your attention on who is speaking; when you are speaking, make sure you look at each person for a few seconds before moving your eyes to the next person. For larger audiences, a good approach is to imagine the room is divided into three sections. For each section, focus your eyes on that area for 3 seconds, then move to the next section; when you come to the final section, return to the first section! Continue this throughout your entire speech or presentation!

How to move your hands: When you're not using your hands, they should rest in front of your body. Many speaking experts will tell you to keep your hands at your sides, but this looks unnatural and robotic for many people. Instead, try holding your hands together (not tight!) and place them around your bellybutton area. When you want to stress a point, focus on a graph in your PowerPoint, etc., use your hands to slowly and gently gesture to that area. It's best to use a gesture with an open hand, flat palm, and fingers together. These types of gestures are called "Gestures for focus." There are other gestures we will learn in Unit 4.

Practice these three points as you do the following Speaking Assignment. Don't worry about your voice right now—just practice your posture, eye contact, and hand placement and gestures.

Speaking Assignment Present your "ME" chart to the class! While you present your chart, remember to check you're your posture, hands, and eyes. After a student has presented his or her chart, other students should give feedback—what did they do well, and what could be improved?

Unit Assignment

Topic: Daily Life

Assignment: Timeline, journal entry, 1-page informal essay, or 2-minute presentation

Talking about what you typically do each day can seem simple and boring, but it is actually a very complex process full of cultural and societal rules, norms, customs, and traditions. Think about an average day in your life, and document what you do. For example, you might write "Wake up, eat breakfast, go to school" to describe your morning routine, but consider these questions:

-Do you sleep in a Western bed or on a futon on the floor?
-Do you usually eat a "Western" breakfast or a traditional one? Who prepares it?
-Do you live with your parents/siblings/grandparents or alone?
-How do you get to school or work—walk, bike, drive or take the local train?

These are just some example questions to get you thinking, so don't answer each question, but instead use them as a guide to write your assignment!

UNIT 2: DAILY LIFE

Vocabulary List

Check the meaning of the words and phrases below. Then use them in the activities in this unit.

1) knowledge

2) belief

3) custom

4) tradition

5) habit

6) community

7) region

8) law

9) organization

10) ethnic group

In this unit, we will be looking at daily life, which, if you did the Unit 1 final assignment, you have discovered is greatly influenced by culture, traditions, and geographic locations. There are also important connections to race, ethnicity, and gender. So, what is race, ethnicity, and gender?

Activity Work alone or with a partner, and write your own definitions of these words. Don't use a dictionary! Use the knowledge and ideas you have to create meanings for these words.

1) *Race* means...

2) *Ethnicity* means...

3) *Gender* means...

Before we start discussing race, ethnicity, and gender, let's review the meaning of *culture* and *society*. Edward B. Tyler (1871) provided the first definition of *culture*:

> *Culture is that complex whole which includes knowledge, belief, arts, law, morals, custom, and any other habits acquired by humans who are members of a society.*

Tyler's (1871) definition is important because many teachers, researchers, and cultural psychologists use this definition to understand and explain the basic meaning of culture. That said, it is important to know that there are many different definitions of culture, so find one that is easy for you to understand.

Society is much easier to define: *A community of people living in a particular country or region, and having shared customs, laws, and organizations.* While most students think of the first part, it is the second part that is vital to the meaning of what is a society—shared customs, laws, and organizations, such as central government and educational institutions, like universities!

Now that we have reviewed these important terms, let's add to them by understanding the meanings of *race, ethnicity*, and *gender*:

- **Race** is each of the major divisions of humankind, having distinct physical characteristics, and sharing the same culture, history, language, etc.

- **Ethnicity** is belonging to a social group that has a common national or cultural tradition. You will often hear the term **ethnic group**, which is a group of people who identify with each other based on common ancestry, as well as social, cultural, and national experiences.

- **Gender** is the state of being male or female, typically used with reference to social and cultural differences rather than biological ones

Many people use the terms "race" and "ethnicity" interchangeably, but this is actually incorrect based on the definitions given above. It is generally agreed by anthropologists that there are three races of the world[1]:

Caucasion:
Skull: Dolicephalic(Long-Head),High forehead,Little supraobital development.
Face: Mainly Leptoproscopic(Narrow)Sometimes Meso- or even Euryproscopic, Neither Facial nor alveolar prognathism occurs except among some archaic peoples.
Nose:Long,narrow,high in both root and bridge.

Mongoloid:
Skull: High incidence of Brachycephaly(Short Round Head)
American Indians while Mongoloid are often Dolicephalic.
Foreheads slightly lower than that of the Caucasoid.
No Supraobital development.
Face: Wide and short, projecting cheek bones, Prognathism rare. Shovel shaped incisors common especialy in Asia.
Nose: Mesorine(Low and Broad in both root and bridge.

Negroid:
Skull: usually Dolicephalic, a small minority are Brachycephalic.
Forehead most often high, little supraobital development.
Face: Leproscopic (to a much lesser degree than the Caucasion), Prognathism common in most Negro populations.
Nose: Low & broad in root and bridge with characteristic depression at root.

Photo taken from https://blog.world-mysteries.com/science/how-many-major-races-are-there-in-the-world/

Considering your race, ethnicity, and gender, let's now look at what daily life looks like where you're originally from and where you are living now. Sometimes these are different, even when they're both the same country! The first thing to do is list as many aspects of daily life as you can.

---

[1] It is <u>important</u> that everyone understands that this information is not *the* "correct" answer, but rather one viewpoint about race, ethnicity, and gender. These stances are meant to be springboards for critical thinking and open discussion. You are encouraged to conduct more research, and decide for yourself what you believe.

Activity Work with a partner, and write some main components that make up daily life. For example, food makes up a huge part of daily life in any country! List your answers below. You can draw simple pictures, too!

After you're finished, look at page 17 and see how many components that you wrote down match the ones in the list of aspects of daily life!

- **Food**
- **Clothing**
- **Recreation**
- **Government**
- **Laws**
- **Education**
- **Language**
- **Habits**
- **Routines**
- **History**
- **Traditions**
- **Religious Beliefs**
- **Transportations**
- **Economy**
- **Daily Spending Habits**
- **Environment**
- **Popular Culture**
- **Art**
- **Music**
- **Social Groups**
- **Sports**
- **Ethnic Groups**

It is interesting to remember that every point in this list can be looked at differently depending on the race, ethnicity, and gender of a person! For example, generally speaking, different regions of the world eat different foods; clothing varies depending on the ethnic group; and sports are different depending on gender (either by choice or defined by cultural rules and traditions, such as sumo in Japan). Our goal is to broaden our perspectives so that we are considering these cultural differences that impact the way we live.

Discussion Questions

1. Describe the average weekday/weekend of the average person in your cultural group. What would a day or weekend look like for an office worker, a housewife, a child in daycare, a high school student, etc.?
2. In small groups, assign roles to each student (working father, housewife, high school student, teacher, homeless person, criminal in prison, or any idea your group might have). Take a few minutes to consider their daily life, and then debate about who has the easiest / most difficult life in society.
3. Reviewing the list you made on page 16 of the various parts of daily life, are there any aspects of daily life in your home country that could be considered negative by those outside your cultural group?

In the previous unit, we discussed using your body in ways that convey a positive, confident message to your listeners. In this unit, we'll be looking at how to use your voice to further convey confidence, but also to add clearness and emphasis! We will look at two points in this unit: clarity and volume.

The first point to remember is to speak clearly. While this sounds easy, it is actually difficult even for native English speakers for many reasons. Two common reasons are: 1) people get nervous when they're speaking, and 2) people think faster than they speak. In both cases, words come out too quickly, and words become connected, and sentences eventually blend into each other. It is important to pronounce each word carefully and speak slowly (but not too slowly!), and don't worry about "sounding fluent" (for non-native speakers) or "sounding persuasive" (two misconceptions about speaking quickly).

The second point to remember, particularly when speaking in a room full of people, is to speak at a level that is louder than your regular speaking voice. Many people become nervous when they speak, especially when they speak in front of an audience, and do not project their voice loud enough to be heard by everyone.

Fortunately, overcoming this speaking issue is pretty easy! First, make sure your posture is correct (from Unit 1). Next, use more air to make your voice louder—not screaming or shouting, but speaking with a stronger, louder tone than you normally would. Practice now: Say "hello" in your regular voice, and then say it again while sitting or standing straight and using more air to make your voice louder. Your second "hello" should sound more deeper and stronger, which helps make you seem surer of what you're saying.

Lastly, the only way to become better at something is to practice, so you have to make many opportunities to speak in front of people. This might be easier for some people, but for those who are shy or timid, it may take more time. Stand in front of a mirror (or face a partner) and practice saying words or expressions over and over. For speeches, memorizing a speech is good practice, but requires more work involving intonation and gestures—two strategies that we'll look at in the next couple of chapters.

Speaking Assignment Take turns standing in front of the class. Check your posture (Unit 1), and practice saying the following in a loud, slow, clear voice:

"Good morning. My name is _____.

I'm a student at _____.

My major is _____.

My hobby is _____.

Thank you."

You do not have to memorize these sentences, and are free to add more information about yourself (for example, the area you live and your desired job after graduating university). The focus should be on posture and voice intonation, volume, and clarity.

Unit Assignment

Topic: Traditions and Beliefs

Assignment: Journal entry, 1-2-page essay, or 2-5-minute presentation

Conduct research on Japanese traditions and beliefs (or the traditions and beliefs from your home country). Take notes while you research so it will be easier to write a paper or discuss the topic in class. Which traditions are embedded in Japanese society? What important beliefs do Japanese people hold? Do these traditions and beliefs come from religion or a historical event? Be prepared to discuss what you've found to a small group and to the class!

UNIT 3: TRADITIONS AND BELIEFS (JAPAN)

Vocabulary List

Check the meaning of the words and phrases below. Then use them in the activities in this unit.

1) traditional

2) modern

3) superstition

4) religion

5) spirituality

6) role

7) child rearing

8) norm

9) collectivism

10) individualism

Up until now, we've looked at culture from an individual perspective and from a country or regional perspective. Cultures can be divided into many categories, but one interesting set of categories is the idea of a *collectivistic society* and an *individualistic society*. This is often referred to as "individualism versus collectivism" because they are opposite ideas.

Hofstede (2020) describes individualism as "a preference for a loosely-knit social framework in which individuals are expected to take care of only themselves and their immediate families," and collectivism as "a preference for a tightly-knit framework in society in which individuals can expect their relatives or members of a particular ingroup to look after them in exchange for unquestioning loyalty." This dichotomy (a division between two different things) is often summarized as "Me" and "We" cultures, and can also include:

Individualist Cultures	Collectivist Cultures
*Focus is on individuality	*Focus us on group harmony
*Individual achievement is stressed	*Group success is stressed
*Personal opinions are voiced	*The concept of "face" is important

Adapted from Hofstede, Hofstede & Minkov (2012)

There are many more characteristics, and some can be argued against, but this information is simply to help you get a better understanding of the concept of individualism and collectivism. There are many videos online that explain individualism versus collectivism, but an interesting one is titled, "Collectivism/Individualism Through Dance" (URL is below the picture).

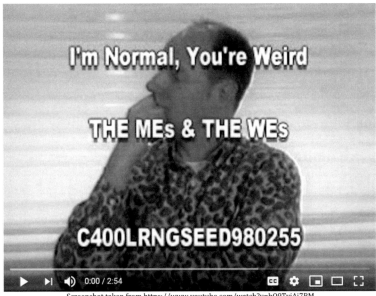

Screenshot taken from https://www.youtube.com/watch?v=bO9TyiAj7BM

21

Although it's a little old, the video briefly explains both concepts, and uses dancing as an example to illustrate their meanings. The video compares a Middle Eastern traditional dance to a more modern style of American dancing. Now, let's compare two different styles of dance and the places where they happen: Rave dancing in America and Bon Festival Dancing in Japan.

Music at raves varies, but it can be generally categorized as Electronic Dance Music (EDM). The dancing that goes along with it also varies, and has several names, such as "shuffling," "Melbourne Shuffle," and "Liquid Dancing." The important point to look at is *how* the dancing is done at raves. Dancing is generally done alone, and is an expression of each individual. It's a time for a person to show his or her uniqueness and individual skill. This actually applies to most raves in Western countries, not just America.

Obon Festival (お盆), on the other hand, is a Japanese Buddhist custom that gives families the opportunity to honor their ancestors. During this time, many families come together to visit and wash family graves before visiting a local festival. It is at this festival where a dance called "bon-odori" (盆踊り) performed. The dance varies from region to region, but essentially a large group of dancers performs the same movements while wearing the same or similar traditional clothing. Many dances tell a story, or depict a regions history or well-known characteristics. Regardless of the region, clothing, and dance moves, the message is the same—everyone dances in unity. This is not the time to show one's unique abilities or bring attention to oneself.

These two dances are one characteristic of individualist cultures and collectivist cultures. There are many other ways to understand individualism and collectivism, but for the sake of this chapter, understanding the general idea is most important. In short, individualist cultures focus on individual success, take care of their own needs before others, and place importance on individual identity; collectivist cultures, on the other hand, focus on group success, take care of each other's needs, and place importance on fitting in rather than expressing unique identities that may go against the group's identity.

Traditions, Customs and Beliefs

In the last unit, we defined *tradition* and *customs.* Your dictionary may have given the same meaning for both, and this is true for many dictionaries, but the reality is that there are subtle differences that need to be understood.

Customs can be viewed as social practices, meaning something that a culture does regularly. Most people in that culture understand it and follow it. For example, when you enter a home in Japan, most Japanese people take off their shoes.

A tradition is similar to a custom, but it has been passed from generation to generation, and it usually changes a little over time. For example, a common way to celebrate Halloween in America is by wearing costumes, but those costumes have changed over the years, from ghosts and witches to famous people and "sexy" versions of almost any character you can think of—even zombies!

To make things more confusing, a tradition can be considered a custom, but not all customs can be considered traditions. Just think about them in relation to time and popularity. If what you're looking at has not lasted a long time, and can be considered a part of a family or individual, it is a custom. Traditions are usually very old, passed to future generations, and many people follow them.

A belief is accepting something as true, or having faith in a way of thinking because it has become a part of your cultural ideology. As you probably guessed, a belief can be religious. Many of Japan's traditions and customs are based in religious beliefs, mainly Shintoism and Buddhism. Beliefs can also be superstitious—stories such as myths or legends containing supernatural beings!

Activity See if you can finish these popular superstitious beliefs from Japan:

- If you whistle at night, ...
- If you lie down after a meal, ...
- The numbers 4 and 7 mean...

Think of three more superstitions from your home culture! What are they, what are their meanings, and where did they come from?

-

-

-

Discussion Questions

1. What modern beliefs are replacing traditional ways of thinking? Discuss this question in general terms (for example, the way holidays are celebrated), as well as specifically in your home country (like the discussion on Halloween in America).

2. As discussed in question 1, many cultures are replacing (or being pressured to replace) old traditions and customs with more modern views. Think of some major changes in your home country. Are these changes being accepted by most people in society (for example, old people, young people, men, women, etc.)? Are such changes viewed as good for society or bad? In what ways?

3. Discuss traditional roles of men and women, and compare them to modern roles. What specifically has changed throughout the years regarding the roles of men and women? Have all of these changes been positive, or have some changes impacted men and/or women in negative ways?

Speaking Strategies: General Speaking Skills, Part III

Now that you've understood the importance of your body when speaking, and hopefully have practiced a lot, then it's time to practice intonation. Intonation is basically how your voice sounds when you're having a conversation—the tone of your voice rises and falls. This rising and falling tone gives our words meaning, and helps our speakers to *feel* what we're saying.

For example, imagine you have a very important test tomorrow. How would you express the importance of this test to your friends? There are many ways!

You can make a word longer: "I have a *huuuuuuuge* test tomorrow." By making the word longer, you place emphasis (or stress) the word, which tells your listener that this is important information. When you make words longer, you usually don't have to explain to the listener how you feel. They'll know!

You can pause before the important word: "I have a ... huge test tomorrow." By pausing before the word, you, again, tell your listener that this is important information.

You can also just put emphasis or stress on a word" "I have a **HUGE** test tomorrow." In other words, make the word or phrase louder than the rest of the sentence.

Let's practice! Remember the Speaking Assignment from Unit 3?

Speaking Assignment Take turns standing in front of a partner. Check your posture (Unit 1), speak in a loud, slow, clear voice (Unit 2), and repeat the following sentences. This time, choose which word you're going to make longer, stronger, or pause before saying:

"Good morning. My name is _____.
I'm a student at _____.
My major is _____.
My hobby is _____.
Thank you."

Unit Assignment

Topic: Collectivist and Individualist Societies

Assignment: Essay or Speech, or Presentation

Choose one of the prompts below, and write an essay or prepare a presentation on that topic.

1) How does living in a collectivist/individualist society affect a person's daily life, traditions, and beliefs? Give examples for each point you make! (Note: Students may choose to present either collectivist or individualist...or do both!)

2) Search online for a traditional or modern dance from Japan or from your home country, and quickly learn a few basic steps. Perform a brief part of the dance (30 seconds-1 minute), and then explain the history of the dance. Are there any traditional instruments used to perform the music? What clothing do dancers wear? Do the movements mean anything?

3) Research the political history and structure of Germany*. Create a timeline of important events. What are some similarities and differences with the Japanese (or your home country) political system?

This last assignment should be completed before starting Unit 4!

UNIT 4: POLITICS (GERMANY)

Vocabulary List

Check the meaning of the words and phrases below. Then use them in the activities in this unit.

1) government

2) politics

3) vote

4) legislation

5) citizen

6) economy

7) conservative

8) liberal

9) democracy

10) (political) party

The goal of this chapter is not to explain what a government is, how it's supposed to work, or what it does, but instead give you the opportunity to talk about the government(s) you are familiar with, your experience with them, and some opinions you might have on certain governments and world leaders. How governments work is difficult to understand, but some form of government can be found in every country around the world, so it is important to learn about.

Before starting our discussion, it is important to understand that in many cultures, it is considered rude to talk about politics, especially personal political affiliations. This might sound confusing, but in a culture that values harmony and friendship, talking about a subject that could potentially cause an argument is not something people want to do, so most people in countries, such as the United States, generally avoid talking about politics in casual settings. Because of controversial government leaders and political scandals, this perspective is slowly changing, but generally this is a good cultural rule to follow.

With that said, let's begin a respectful discussion on politics in Germany. Remember to consider the structure of the government and how it generally functions, but also keep in mind important historical events. For example, World War I and World War II are deeply connected to global governments, political figures, national and international laws, and many other aspects of politics as a field of study.

Activity What do you know about governments and politics? Get into small groups, and take turns sharing what you now! If you did the homework from Unit 3's Assignment (Question #3), you can use your notes and timelines. Write your group's answers in the space below.

Germany

Germany has a long history that is deeply connected to its government and political leaders. Of course, everyone knows a little about World War II and Adolf Hitler, but what has happened since then? How has Germany recovered from the aftermath of war, and how is the country run now?

A quick way to understand Germany's government is to watch this video explaining generally how it works. (Note: Your instructor may choose not to show this video in class, so watch it on your own before class. Check the URL below the image or search the internet for more information.)

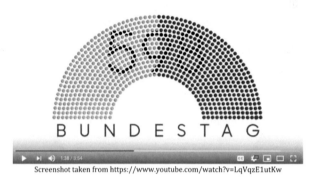

Screenshot taken from https://www.youtube.com/watch?v=LqVqzE1utKw

If there's no chance to watch the video, here is some brief information about Germany's government. Germany has a federal parliamentary democratic republic. That means the government is elected by the people in elections, and everyone has an equal vote. They have a constitution that states the rights of the people, and it also describes the jobs of the President, the Cabinet, the Bundestag and Bundesrat (the two parts of Parliament), and the Courts. The President is the head of state, but this is mostly ceremonial. The Federal Chancellor is actually the head of the government.

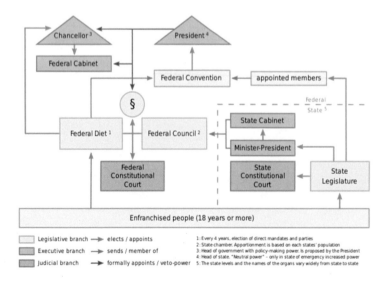

Political System of Germany, Retrieved from https://commons.wikimedia.org/wiki/File:Political_System_of_Germany.svg

Activity Think about the government in your native country (or a country you're familiar with), and look at the table on page 30. For each point in the Germany section, write an equivalent point for your country's government. For instance, the name of Germany's political leader is "chancellor," so the leader from Japan, for example, would be "prime minister," and the leader from the United States would be "president." Another example would be when a country's citizens vote. For Germany, citizens vote for the Bundestag (i.e., federal elections) every four years. When does your country's citizens vote? General information is ok! Don't worry about being exact—the point is to gain a general understanding of how some governments work.

	Germany	Your Country:
1		
2		
3		
4		
5		

Discussion Questions

1. What is your general opinion about local and national governments? Do you think that governments take care of their country's citizens? In what ways do they do, and in what ways do they not?

2. How does your country's government view "hot topics," such as medical care, homeless veterans, and immigration? What other topics are currently being discussed or debated in your country?

3. What are your thoughts on the relationship between the United States and Japan (or any two countries that were once at war but now work together)? Consider difficult topics, such as past wars, conflicts/disputes with other nations, and the current controversy over American military bases in Japan

In Unit 1, you learned about "Gestures for Focus." These are simple movements with your hands and arms that help the audience know what information (on the board, PowerPoint, etc.) you're talking about by drawing attention to that area.

In this unit, we'll learn to use gestures for another important reason: "Gestures for Expression." These physical expressions help the audience understand key points you are talking about in your speech or presentation. Here are a few Gestures for Expression you can use in your speech or presentation, but remember that these gestures could also be used when you're engaged in a regular conversation with a friend, teacher or coworker!

Use "Gestures for Expression" when you want to emphasize:

Numbers: This is the simplest gesture that accompanies words. When you say "one," hold up one finger; when you say "two," hold up two fingers. Be mindful of cultural differences, though! Many cultures have different ways of counting, so make sure you are counting the usual way people do in the area you're currently in. Gesturing while speaking numbers puts the emphasis on the number, and can help your audience keep track of the points you're making. We'll practice this soon.

Sizes (including distances): Again, this is a simple gesture, but is incredibly important when stressing the size of something. Words like small, short, long, tall, and thick are good words to use when describing people or things, but showing the size with your hands can help your audience picture in their minds exactly what you're trying to express. If you say, "He's short," your listener will wonder just how short the person is; but if you say this while showing with your hand how short the person is, it will give your listener the perfect "picture" in their mind of his height.

Importance: Sometimes you really need to emphasize a word or point in order to give your audience a strong impression. The easiest and most natural way to do this is making your voice a little stronger when you say the word, but at the same time striking one of your hands with the other hand. First, place your left (or right) hand in front of you with your palm up (as if you are going to receive change from a cashier). Next, make a fist with your right (or left) hand, and hit the palm of your left hand while you speak the word you're trying to stress. An alternative to a fist would be a "karate chop" strike! Both are effective ways to show your audience that this word is important, and they should remember it.

Speaking Activity Stand up and face a partner. Before you speak, check each other's posture. Next, repeat the following sentences while practicing the gestures above:

"Good morning. My name is _____.
I'm a student at _____.
My major is _____.
I chose this major for *two* reasons" (hold two fingers up). "First, there are *many* students in this department" (make a gesture to show something is big).
"Second, there is a *need* for more _____"
(strike your palm with your fist as you say "need").

Make sure you practice this exercise 3-4 times with your partner! It is very important that you time the words with the gestures so they happen at the same time.

Unit Assignment

Topic: Politics and Religion

Assignment: Essay, debate or presentation.

In many countries, there is a belief in the separation of "church and state," meaning religion or religious groups should not be involved in or influence politics or government (and vice versa). Think of some pros and cons of religion and politics being separate, and present/argue one side.

If you need ideas, there is an interesting article from Time Magazine titled "The Real Meaning of the Separation of Church and State" (http://time.com/5103677/church-state-separation-religious-freedom/) or do an internet search for "separation of church and state."

UNIT 5: RACE AND ETHNICITY (RUSSIA)

Vocabulary List

Check the meaning of the words and phrases below. Then use them in the activities in this unit.

1) history

2) ethnic group

3) diverse

4) population

5) (cultural/ethnic) minority

6) to get along (with)

7) research

8) dialect

9) artifact

10) conflict

In previous chapters, you learned new vocabulary terms related to global cultures and societies, and had many opportunities to discuss, present, and debate topics related to these terms. In this unit, we will expand upon two small terms that have massive impacts in the world today: *ethnicity* and *race*.

Many people, and even some textbooks, use the terms *race* and *ethnicity* as interchangeably, but, as you now know, they are very different. Ethnicity is a group that has a common national and cultural background. Race, on the other hand, is the major divisions of people in the world, and you saw one example that contained three divisions (remember that there are other theories out there, so choose the one you believe in).

There are many wonderful artifacts, traditions, and beliefs that are created by different ethnic groups, but not all ethnic groups get along with each other. As a matter of fact, many wars and other types of violence have happened because different ethnic groups held different opinions or beliefs. There is also a lot of tension between races, the most famous being between "blacks and whites," and this tension has produced a lot of hatred, mistrust, and violence around the world.

Diversity, or having a lot of variety, is something that is usually viewed as positive, especially when considering racial and ethnic diversity. Some countries, like the United States and Canada, are very racially and ethnically diverse, while other countries, such as Japan and South Korea, are not. Whether diversity has more merits for a country than demerits will be discussed later. For now, let's look at a very large country with an extremely diverse ethnic population—Russia.

Russia

According to the Central Intelligence Agency (2019) World Factbook, Russia's size, about 17.1 square kilometers, makes it the largest country in the world, with an estimated population of about 142 million people.

With regards to the ethnic groups in Russia, here is the breakdown:

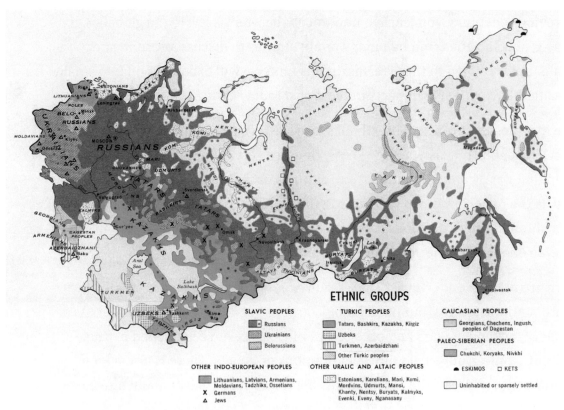

Map taken from https://alphahistory.com/russianrevolution/russian-revolution-maps/

Russian 77.7%

Tatar 3.7%

Ukrainian 1.4%

Bashkir 1.1%

Chuvash 1%

Chechen 1%

other 10.2%

unspecified 3.9% (Central Intelligence Agency (2019)

The map above shows how the various ethnic groups are spread throughout Russia. Take a moment and examine the map before moving on to the next activity.

Activity: Work with a small group, and think about some important characteristics that make ethnic groups unique, and discuss them in detail. You don't have to be a part of a small ethnic group to recognize characteristics. Look at your own cultural group's characteristics, such as customs, habits, traditions, holidays, activities, food preferences, religious beliefs, and language dialects. You can also bring up any experiences you have had with different ethnic groups while you were traveling or studying abroad! Based on these unique characteristics, why would it be difficult for other ethnic groups to get along with them? Try to come up with five, and write them below.

Important characteristic of ethnic groups	Why could this be an issue for other ethnic groups?
1.	
2.	
3.	
4.	
5.	

Based on Russia's 2010 census, there are nearly 200 national and/or ethnic groups in the country! However, there are still many conflicts between ethnic groups, so much that Russia created the "Federal Strategy on Ethnic Conflict Resolution," although apparently it hasn't been very effective in calming tensions between groups (Sewell, 2013).

This unit is not meant to be a history lesson, and if you don't fully understand the situation in Russia, or even in your own home country (assuming it's not Russia), that is ok because the goal is to have a basic understanding of how diverse a large country can be, and how difficult it can be for people in certain groups to get along with other groups. This is a basic problem in society that many countries are dealing with now, and it can extend to other groups, as well: racial, ethnic, gender, sexual preference, socioeconomic, religious, and many others.

Discussion Questions

1. What ethnic groups are in your home country? Are there conflicts between ethnic groups? Why or why not?
2. Would the world be a better place if ethnic identities were no longer acknowledged and celebrated? What would the future look like if there were one ethnicity—a global ethnicity? Would that stop wars from occurring?
3. Think about the other groups listed at the end of the unit. How can you apply what you learned in this unit to those groups? Choose one group to talk about in detail, and use examples to support your ideas!

Speaking Strategies: Cultural Point

In the last units, you learned a lot about using your body, eyes, voice, and hands to send various messages to your audience. In this unit, we will look at how gestures may be used within and across different cultures!

In Unit 2, we looked at "Gestures of Focus," which help speakers show which words and phrases are important. In other words, by speaking a word or phrase and using your hands to, for example, point at that word, you are telling the audience, "This is important, so remember it!"

In Unit 4, we studied "Gestures for Expression," which makes what a speaker saying more vivid to listeners. In other words, your voice and your hands "paint a picture" in audience members' minds, and this helps them better understand what you are trying to say.

In this unit, gestures are looked at from a cultural perspective—so this is more of a cultural lesson than a speaking strategy. According to recent research, where you are from determines how you tell a story (Nicoladis, Nagpal, Marentette, & Hauer, 2019). There are two parts to telling a story. The first part has to do with how a person presents the order to the listener. In Asian countries, the focus tends to be more on the lesson one can learn from the story; in Western countries, the story is told in chronological order (in other words, from the beginning to the middle to the end).

While this information may not seem important to speaking, it is actually extremely important! First, if you understand this information, then you can begin to look at how *you* tell a story. Do you use your hands to show emotions or turmoil within the story, or do you let the moral of the story dominate? Do you start at the beginning of a story and follow the events in order, or do you stress the importance of understand the moral or lesson to be learned? Second, if you understand how different cultures tend to tell stories, then you can be more mindful of your storyteller, and therefore more sensitive to his or her culture's way of presenting a tale. In short, knowing that "culture/language groups differ in story-telling style" will help you be a culturally-sensitive listener (Nicoladis, Nagpal, Marentette, & Hauer, 2019).

Speaking Assignment Think of a famous story, legend, fable or fairytale from your culture. Write down some notes detailing the important parts of the story. What is the setting (where and what time does the story take place)? Who are the main characters? How does the story evolve (beginning, middle, and end)? Are there any lessons to be learned from the story? What parts of your culture are highlighted or stressed in the story, characters, and/or lessons?

Use the box below to record your notes about your chosen story! Feel free to draw pictures of the setting, main characters, important items, and/or maps to help illustrate your story!

When you are ready, form small groups of 3-4 students, and take turns telling stories. Don't think about gestures or your voice—tell the story as naturally as possible. After you are finished, have the other group members (the listeners) tell you how they noticed your hands moving, voice changing, etc. as you told different parts of the story!

Unit Assignment

Topic: Ethnic Minorities

Assignment: Debate (strongly recommended for this activity, but a presentation, or academic essay would also be possible)

An *ethnic minority* is a group of people from one culture who live in a country where most of the people are from a different culture (in other words, they are the ethnic majority). Ethnic minorities can be found in every country all over the world. An example would be the Ainu people in Japan (for more information on the Ainu, visit http://www.ainu-museum.or.jp/en/).

Split the classroom into two large groups. One group will be the ethnic majority and the other group will be the ethnic minority. You will not choose a country or ethnic group! You will simply be the "minority" and "majority" of an unnamed country.

The **ethnic minority group** will create ten (10) changes that they want the ethnic majority to make in order for both groups to be equal. Right now, they are not equal in many ways. For example, job promotions, university scholarships, and housing in good neighborhoods are difficult to get for minority members.

The **ethnic majority group** will have to come up with reasons to oppose each request. Your goal is to protect the ethnic majority's interests.

20 minutes: Preparation time for each group.

10 minutes: Debate (The **ethnic minority group** presents one change, followed by a rebuttal by the **ethnic majority group**. Continue until all changes are presented and challenged).

10 minutes: Classroom discussion. How did you feel being part of each group?

Remember: You are not trying to highlight how unfair ethnic majorities can be to ethnic minorities, or how ethnic minorities can cause issues in society. The goal of this debate is not to fight, argue or "point fingers" (i.e., blame each other for problems you have), but to go through a debate *in order to* understand both sides of an ethnic group dispute. You don't have to agree with one or the other— you simply have to gain a better understanding.

Understanding perspectives from other cultures can help us grow as Global Critical Thinkers (GCT) (Velasco, 2018)!

UNIT 6: GENDER (UNITED STATES)

Vocabulary List

Check the meaning of the words and phrases below. Then use them in the activities in this unit.

1) sex (in contrast to *gender*)

2) cultural

3) biological

4) LGBT+

5) gender gap

6) inequality

7) gender role

8) gender equal

9) attain

10) empowerment

There are many topics to consider when studying gender. It is an important topic that has become more relevant and complex with issues like gender equality, same-sex marriage, and sexual identity being hotly debated in countries all around the world. With powerful movements like #MeToo, socially accepted changes like gender-neutral restrooms, and controversial accusations toward famous and powerful people, it is impossible not to consider gender as a global social and cultural issue that is a critical topic to study.

A sign for a gender-neutral bathroom in the United States.

Regarding increasing our Global Critical Thinking (GCT) and intercultural communication skills, one area that needs to be explored first is the gap between genders across the world. When the gap is wider, that means that country has unfair treatment policies between women and men.

How can we measure such treatment? The Global Gender Gap Report (World Economic Forum, 2018) does just that! The Global Gender Gap Report is a list of countries and their global ranking regarding the disparity (or imbalance) between males and females. The ranking is based on four areas:

- economic participation and opportunity
- educational attainment
- health and survival
- political empowerment

Do women and men both work? If so, do they hold similar positions in various businesses and organizations? If so, are there equal chances for promotion into higher-level positions, or is it more difficult for women to gain higher status positions? What about owning businesses? Are women and men able to start a business, and receive support, such as bank loans?

Attainment, as you discovered from your vocabulary list, means succeeding in achieving or accomplishing something that you wanted. Education attainment, therefore, means the ability to receive an education. In some countries, women have equal chances to receive an education, including receiving benefits, such as scholarships from their government or school. For others, it is extremely difficult and, in some cases, impossible to receive an education. Depending on the area, seeking out an education can be dangerous!

How healthy are men compared to women? Are there big differences in the health services that are available for both men and women? What is the survival rate for male and female babies?

Finally, politics have been dominated by men for centuries. How much do women participate in local and national politics? For some countries, women have become the political leaders, and have proven that they are just as capable as men of holding positions of power and authority. For other countries, unfortunately, women do not have many (if any at all) chances to join political groups and hold government offices.

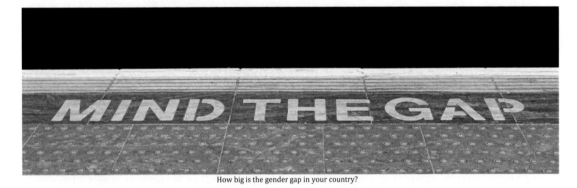

How big is the gender gap in your country?

Activity Before looking at the list, think of the country where you were born. How do you think this country scores in these four areas? For each one, write a few examples of how the country does a good job or a poor job at supporting equality between men and women. After you finish writing comments and examples, rank that area from 1-10 (1=poor, 5=ok, but could improve, 10=excellent).

When you've completed all four, guess what ranking the country you chose received in the Global Gender Gap Index.

When you're finished with everything, share your chart with a partner or small group!

Country: _____

Areas	Comments & Examples	Rank
economic participation and opportunity		
educational attainment		
health and survival		
political empowerment		
GLOBAL RANKING	***WHAT RANKING DO YOU THINK THIS COUNTRY RECEIVED?***	

Global Gender Gap Report 2020

Now it's time to look at the rankings! Here are the top 10 countries in the 2020 Global Gender Gap Report (The full report can be viewed at http://www3.weforum.org/docs/WEF_GGGR_2020.pdf).

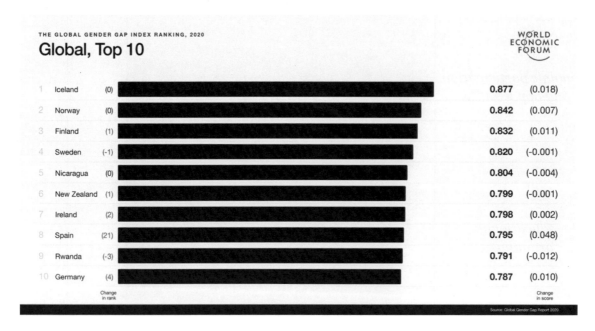

Here is a chart focused on The United States:

	2006 score		2020 score	
Global Gender Gap Index	23	0.704	53	0.724
Economic participation and opportunity	3	0.759	26	0.756
Educational attainment	66	0.982	34	1.000
Health and survival	1	0.980	70	0.976
Political empowerment	66	0.097	86	0.164

▬▬ United States score

— average score

To put the scores into a "West versus East" (or individualist versus collectivist) perspective, here is Japan's ranking:

44

Japan

	2006 score		2020 score	
Global Gender Gap Index	80	0.645	121	0.652
Economic participation and opportunity	83	0.545	115	0.598
Educational attainment	60	0.986	91	0.983
Health and survival	1	0.980	40	0.979
Political empowerment	83	0.067	144	0.049

▬▬ Japan score

— average score

What do all these rankings mean? According to the Global Gender Gap Report, "In 2020, the Global Gender Gap score (based on the population-weighted average) stands at 68.6%. This means that, on average, the gap is narrower, and the remaining gap to close is now 31.4%" (World Economic Forum, 2020, p. 8). In short, ranking countries by how large or small the gap is between genders will help decrease the gap, making all countries better places to work, live, and thrive for both men and women!

Progress to close the gender gaps is slow, though, and while some countries have moved up in the ranking, others have fallen. Also, countries that are modern, technologically advanced, and claim to offer fair opportunities to women, like the United States and Japan, are ranked low in the list. But why? Let's talk about it!

Discussion Questions

1. Which country ranking surprised you the most? Which surprised you the least? Why?
2. Look at the list and rankings that you created in the activity above, and compare them to the actual ranking by the World Economic Forum. What are the differences? How do you feel about your country's ranking?
3. Do you believe gender equality will ever be achieved globally? Why or why not? What are some specific obstacles that are hindering gender equality?

In Unit 5, you had the opportunity to be involved in a formal debate—"formal" meaning there were two sides, and it was organized in some way. In this section, we will begin to look at some basic debate skills.

First, what is a debate, and why are debate skills important? A debate is not a passionate fight or an angry challenge, but a controlled, respectful argument for or against a certain issue that is usually viewed as controversial in some way. People who are in a debate use reasons, examples, and statistics to prove their point in order to persuade a group of pcople who are judging the debate, or audience members. What differentiates debates and regular arguments? There are rules that debaters must follow!

A good example of these rules is the structure of debates. Let's look at one common format for a debate. Imagine there are two teams with two members each. Team A is "for" an idea (pro) and the Team B is "against" (con). Here is one way the debate can be formatted:

Team/Speaker #	What to present	Time to present
Team A / Speaker 1	Introduces the topic, and presents the team's first argument.	5 minutes
Team B / Speaker 2	Presents the team's first argument.	5 minutes
Team A / Speaker 1	Presents the team's second argument.	5 minutes
Team B / Speaker 2	Presents the team's second argument.	5 minutes
	BREAK (Both teams prepare rebuttal statements)	5-10 minutes
Team B / Speaker 1 & 2	Both speakers present their team's rebuttal statement to Team A's two points. After, they summarize their main points.	10 minutes
Team A / Speaker 1 & 2	Both speakers present their team's rebuttal statement to Team A's two points. After, they summarize their main points.	10 minutes

Speaking Activity Make two teams with two classmates on each team. Decide which team is A and which is B. Next, choose a type of sandwich (for example, ham & cheese versus peanut butter & jelly) or a writing instrument (pen versus pencil)—something simple and easy to support. Remember that you are not trying to "win," but simply practice the debate structure. After, make a quick list with your partner of strong points about your chosen item. For example, if you chose a pencil (and the opposite team chose pen), you could point out that pencils are better because a writer can erase what he or she has written, making mistakes unnoticeable on a paper. Use the chart below to structure your mini-debate!

Team/Speaker #	What to present	Time to present	Notes
Team A / Speaker 1	Introduce the topic, and present your team's first argument.	1 minute	
Team B / Speaker 2	Present your team's first argument.	1 minute	
Team A / Speaker 1	Presents your team's second argument.	1 minute	
Team B / Speaker 2	Presents your team's second argument.	1 minute	
	BREAK (Both teams prepare rebuttal statements)	2 minutes	
Team B / Speaker 1 & 2	Both speakers present your team's rebuttal statement to Team A's two points. After, summarize their main points.	1 minute	
Team A / Speaker 1 & 2	Both speakers present your team's rebuttal statement to Team A's two points. After, summarize their main points.	1 minute	

After you have finished your debate, talk about the process with both teams. How was this different from a usual argument between two people? What are some strengths to debating? How can debating skills be used in regular conversations?

Unit Assignment

Topic: To be or not to be...a housewife!

Assignment: Roundtable discussion, debate or reflection paper (in-class or homework)

Before starting the assignment, view the video titled, **"Do Japanese Girls Want to be a Housewife (Interview)"** posted by Japanese YouTuber *That Japanese Man Yuta* (URL: https://www.youtube.com/watch?v=zWLSSk8H4sc). Your teacher can play the video on the classroom projector, or allow you to watch it on your laptop, smartphone or tablet. (Note: Your teacher may also choose *not* to play the video. If the video will not be used, you can still complete the three assignments listed below.)

During the video, take notes so you'll remember important points. If the video won't be used, write down some of your home country's views on housewives. After, your teacher will decide which assignments the class will do from the options below.

Option A

The entire class should sit in a circle (the "roundtable") so everyone is facing each other. When everyone is seated with their notes, have a conversation about the points that were made in the video, your home country's views on housewives, and/or your personal opinions about housewives (or stay-at-home mothers).

48

Make sure that each person speaks at least once, and talks about the three areas listed above!

Option B

Divide the class into two teams. Decide which team encourages women to be housewives and which team discourages women to be housewives. Use the chart from the Speaking Activity to guide your response times.

Remember that you don't have to really *believe* "all women should be housewives"! Think of reasons why some people *would* believe that—for example, some reasons presented in the video, or reasons from your home country—and present them in the debate. <u>No one should get upset by any comments that are made</u>! This is just an exercise to practice expressing ideas and opinions in a debate format.

Option 3

Write about both sides of this argument? Why do some countries encourage women to stay home and be "housewives," and others view being a housewife as a form of slavery or subservience (in other words, obeying others without questioning their authority)? Write a one-page reflection essay (either in-class or at home), and prepare to discuss what you wrote in the next class.

UNIT 7: RELIGION (ITALY)

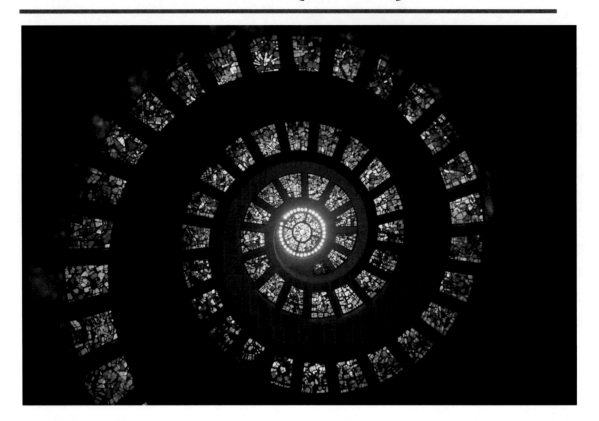

Vocabulary List

Check the meaning of the words and phrases below. Then use them in the activities in this unit.

1) religion

2) spirituality

3) agnostic

4) Christianity

5) Islam

6) cult

7) ceremony

8) stereotypes

9) crusade

10) extremism

Religion is a topic that people have been pondering, discussing, debating, romanticizing, and philosophizing since the beginning of humanity (and maybe even before that). Religion, spirituality, and in some ways even agnosticism and atheism, have encouraged, inspired, and saved millions of people's lives, but it also has hurt, defeated, and destroyed just as many lives. It has caused people to sit alone in caves for years, sell all their possessions and travel to foreign lands, incite wars, write books, give speeches, marry, divorce, wear certain clothing, shave their heads, grow long beards, and sit under freezing cold waterfalls.

At this point, a gentle (cultural) warning should be given:

The subject of religion is far to vast and complex to adequately cover in this textbook, and it is an extremely difficult topic for many people to discuss. It is very important that everyone's mind remains open and flexible to other ideas and ways. The goal is never to change people, but to listen, respect, and understand their perspective. This, as mentioned in a previous unit, is how we become better intercultural communicators and Global Critical Thinkers.

With that said, for the purposes of reflection and discussion, let's take a look at some general information about religion, and move into our focus of Italy.

How many religions are there in the world? Answers vary from source to source, but I think there is one that seems to give a pretty acceptable response. According to Barrett, et al., (2001), there are 19 major world religions in the world, which are subdivided into a total of 270 large religious groups, and many smaller ones. For example, 34,000 separate Christian groups have been identified in the world.

Christians are the largest religious group in 2015

% of world population

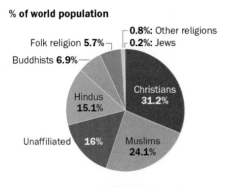

Number of people in 2015, in billions

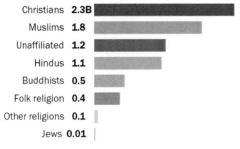

Pew Research Center, 2017

The pie chart above shows the percentages of major world religions, although the pie chart's percentages provide only a "snapshot" of the general religious categories. The numbers are also based on information from several years ago, but it should be noted that the percentages in the categories (mainly Christianity and Islam) fluctuate only slightly. In the map below, you can see how the major religions are spread out in every region around the world (PBS, 2020).

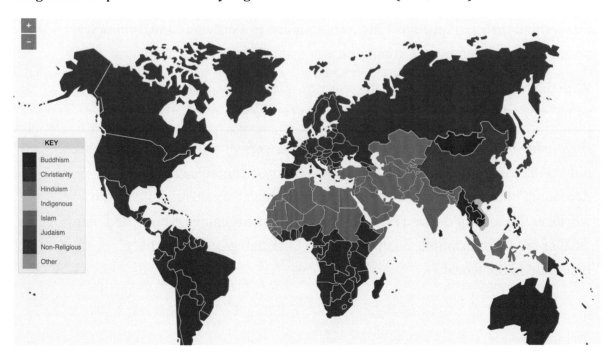

If you are unfamiliar with any of the religions listed above, that's ok! Although most people have probably heard of the major religions in the world, many of them are not familiar with their belief systems, customs, and traditions, which means that a lot of what they believe is based on stereotypes. Stereotypes, or false beliefs based on a small amount of truth, can be very dangerous. Some examples of religious stereotypes are "All Muslims are terrorists," "Buddhists have no emotions or feelings," and "All Christians are judgmental and hypocritical."

Activity Which religion is considered the "major" religion in your home country? What are some main features of the religion? For example, does the religion have one god, many gods or no gods? What are the stereotypes associated with this religion? For example, if your home country's main religion is Buddhist, you could write something like, "All Buddhists shave their heads and meditate." Remember that a stereotype is an exaggerated belief that is based on some truth (in other words, *some* Buddhists may shave their heads and meditate, but not *all* of them). After you have written some information in the chart below, share with a partner or small group!

KEEP IN MIND: You don't have to talk about your or your family's religious beliefs, although you are welcome to discuss them if you and your partner/group are comfortable with each other and respectful of each other's ideas and perspectives. If you're not sure, just talk about your country's main religion in general.

Home Country's Main Religion	Main Features	Stereotypes

Italy

When one thinks of "Italy" and "religion," it is almost impossible not to think about the Pope—the Bishop of Rome, and the head of the Roman Catholic

Church. If you review the chart below, you can see that Christianity is the religion of the majority of Italy—83.3% of the population of Italy, to be exact!

The Religious Demographics Of Italy

Rank	Religion	Number Of Believers	% of Population
1	Christianity	43,433,750	71.4
2	Islam	1,859,100	3.1
3	Buddhism	257,300	0.4
4	Hinduism	177,200	0.3
5	Sikhism	150,000	0.2
6	Judaism	42,850	0.1

World Atlas, 2020

Although the second largest religious group, Islam is only around 3% of the population, but are many concerns and challenges behind this small number. Muslims make up 3% of Italy's population, but Islam is not a legally recognized religion in Italy, and there is only one mosque that provides a place for prayer for one million Muslims.

Activity If possible, first view the video titled "One million Muslims, one mosque" in class (RT News, 2008) (URL: https://www.youtube.com/watch?v=xb0wmui7hTE).

Work with a partner or small group, and discuss both sides to this argument. What do both sides want, and, perhaps more importantly, what do both sides fear?

Muslims in Italy	Those Against Muslims in Italy

For additional information, watch the video, "Islam second largest religion in Italy but still unrecognized" (PressTV, 2016) (URL: https://www.youtube.com/watch?v=cpPwG4sZcyE).

Both videos illustrate the problems Muslims are experiencing in Italy, and how the Italian government is making religious activities difficult for them. After you watch the videos, return to your lists above and see what is included and what is missing.

Given the information that is available, is Italy's hesitancy with Islam understandable? Consider this question before moving on to the discussion questions below.

As the world becomes smaller due to globalization and technology, one would think that religious understanding and tolerance would increase. However, many events that have taken place or are currently taking place (e.g., new leaders of countries with strong opinions about immigration; refugees seeking new lives and opportunities in foreign countries, racial and religious violence, and so on) have caused a major challenge to global harmony. This is something that every person in every country needs to think about very deeply, and discuss openly with others. Whether you share the same or different opinions, everyone should strive to understand each other, and respect and celebrate cultural, racial, ethnic, and religious differences.

Discussion Questions

1. What are the main religions in your home country? Describe them (history, symbols, traditions, customs, clothing, make-up, gender roles, dance, food, etc.).

2. Think of someone you know who is religious or non-religious (for example, your parents/grandparents/guardians/friends)? How have their beliefs impacted their lives and the lives of those around them?

3. Why is it so difficult for religions to "get along"? Considering all the information in this unit (and what you know from your home country, the media, etc.), is Italy's hesitancy with Islam understandable? What's the situation in your home country?

Speaking Strategies: Debate Skills, Part II

In the previous unit, you learned about the reasons why debate skills are useful, as well as one standard way to hold a debate. In this unit, we'll focus on a few specific skills you should keep in mind while debating.

Attitude: The purpose of a debate is to persuade, or convince, your opponent(s) and audience to agree with your point of view, strategy or opinion about a certain topic. Your debate will not be successful unless you present yourself in a positive, confident, and persuasive way. These three key points can be easily achieved in one way—knowledge. Simply speaking, if you know what you're talking about, and have a lot of information about your opponent's arguments, then you will feel more confident in what you are saying, and, therefore, more persuasive.

Rhythm: Many people believe that a "fast talker" is a convincing talker, but the opposite is actually true! The faster a person talks, the more unsure and untrustworthy they may sound. You are not selling car insurance door-to-door, so take your time when presenting your main points. Speak slowly so everyone can understand you, but not too slow—remember, there is usually a time keeper who is making sure you complete your thoughts before a certain time is up.

Tone: Like a previous unit explained, your voice can provide more information to your listeners. Make sure your voice sounds firm and confident, not angry or frustrated. Change your tone to soften when you're talking about sensitive matters, and stronger when you're talking about important issues that need to be stressed.

Volume: How loud or quiet your voice should largely depend on the size of the room you're in, as well as the topic you're debating. Shouting never won any debates, but neither have whispers. A good rule is to speak at 150% (100% being your regular voice you use to talk to friends or order food from a restaurant). Adjust your volume according to the size of the room, how many people are in the room, and other factors (such as microphones being used).

Pronunciation: Practicing pronunciation, even for native English speakers, is a requirement before speaking in public. You want to be sure every word is understood, so speak slowly, clearly, and concisely. Learn your culture's pronunciation "trouble spots" (for example, how the "l," "r," and "th-" sounds are pronounced by Japanese speakers).

Eye contact: Another key point that was made in a previous unit is the important of eye contact. One way to ensure you won't be reading pre-written scripts is to simply not have them. Notes on small index cards can be helpful, but avoid writing full sentences on them. Nobody wants to watch you read a piece of paper like a robot, so practice your speech and only use index cards if absolutely necessary.

Take notes: Lastly, take notes when you are not speaking. If your partner is speaking, write down what she or he is saying, as well as how the other team or even some audience members responded to anything mentioned. This could help you adjust your next speech and hopefully get your message across clearly and effectively!

Speaking Activity With one partner, practice reading through your lists from above (or from another issue that that you and your partner are familiar with). No one is trying to "win" the debate, so just practice the suggestions given above, and then give each other feedback on how to improve your debate skills.

Unit Assignment

Topic: Poster Presentation, in-class essay, journal entry

Assignment: Describe your last "religious" or "spiritual" experience or encounter. Perhaps you have encountered someone knocking on your apartment door on a Sunday evening, and you realized you were talking to a cult member or a Jehovah's Witness solicitor who was trying to get you to join one of their gatherings. Or, maybe you once attended a Japanese festival, and participated in carrying the *mikoshi* (神輿 or portable shrine). Watching a movie, such as Martin Scorsese's film *Silence* (a movie about the first Christians in Japan) could also be considered a religious experience. Have you ever read a religious book, such as The Bible or Quran, or a book about religions, such as a textbook for a World Religions college course? This could also be considered a religious or spiritual event!

How did you feel before, during, and after the event? Did it change the way you viewed another religious, spiritual, and/or historical event? In what ways was culture expressed in this event?

UNIT 8: EDUCATION (PAKISTAN)

Vocabulary List

Check the meaning of the words and phrases below. Then use them in the activities in this unit.

1) institution

2) reform

3) literacy

4) diploma / degree

5) disparity

6) urban / rural

7) socioeconomic

8) vocational school

9) academic

10) disproportionate

59

Education, like many topics in this textbook, can mean different things to different people. For some people, education is a way to escape poverty or violent crime; for others, it is something that every person has a right to receive. A "life education" (experiences received "on the street," traveling or working) may be just as valuable as an academic one.

Where one is born and raised also influences how education is viewed. In some communities, high academic credentials, such as master degrees (MA, MEd, MSc) and doctoral degrees (PhD, PsyD, EdD), are recognized and celebrated, while in other areas, such as poor and rural areas, vocational training may provide stable long-term income, and therefore be seen as more valuable. All training and experiences are important, and no one can say that a person with a PhD is more or less important than someone who has trained to be an electrician.

Activity Think about the area or community where you were born and raised. What types of education are available, who are they available to, and how are graduates viewed by the people in that community? For example, there might be a dental school in your area, but the tuition is expensive and there are limited scholarships, so most of the students are from the middle-class; graduates from this school may be able to get the best jobs in the area or have the opportunity to move to a larger city, so they earn respect from the community. What about your area or community? Describe three types of educational institutions below.

My Area/Community: _____

Types of Education	Who can go?	How are graduates viewed?	Additional Comments

After you have finished your chart, share your responses with a partner or small group. Are there any areas of the world that are similar? What are the main differences?

Pakistan

Pakistan has a long, rich history that dates back thousands of years. The country has gone through many dynasties, empires, invasions, and even a period of colonization by the British. Pakistan became independent tin 1947, and since then there have been many difficulties, including difficulties with their education system. Peter Blood (1994) wrote, "At independence, Pakistan had a poorly educated population and few schools or universities. Although the education system has expanded greatly since then, debate continues about the curriculum, and, except in a few elite institutions, quality remained a crucial concern of educators." Adult literacy is low, the government does not invest a lot of money in education, and certain groups hinder the efforts of some who are trying to get an education.

Traditionally, in many areas of the world, education was given to boys, while the girls were prepared for a life taking care of the home and raising children. Times have changed, and globalization has impacted even rural villages across the world. Pakistan is in crisis right now for many reasons, but one may be that times are moving too quickly, and change is not easily accepted. Naviwala (2017) writes,

> Foreign donors also want Pakistanis to send their girls to schools, but a 2014 Pew survey found that 86 percent of Pakistanis believe that education is equally important for boys and girls, while another 5 percent said it was more important for girls. Even in the northwestern province of Khyber Pakhtunkhwa — where Malala Yousafzai is from — government high schools for girls are enrolled beyond their capacity.

Malala. You've probably heard of her from the news a few years ago, or maybe you've even read her book. Briefly, Malala stood up for her belief in education for women and children, and in return received death threats from the Taliban who were ruling the area at that time, culminating in a failed assassination attempt. Not only did Malala recovery from the bullet that entered her head, but she became even stronger and vocal about women's rights.

Besides the radical changes that Malala's brave story have inspired, more positive news is coming out of Pakistan, with organizations like USAID (2019) building or rehabilitating 946 schools (including the Women's College in Orakzai) and supported reading programs for over 658,500 students in the Tribal Districts of Khyber Pakhtunkhwa (where Malala is from).

Activity With a partner or small group, read the following quote:

"When the whole world is silent, even one voice becomes powerful."
-Malala Yousafzai

First, discuss the meaning of this quote. Next, answer this quick survey:

From 1st grade to now, how satisfied are you with your education? (circle one)

Not at all satisfied   Slightly Satisfied   Neutral   Very Satisfied   Extremely Satisfied

      ☹   ☺   ☺

If you answered between "Neutral" and "Not at all Satisfied," how hard would you fight to change and improve your education? If you answered "Very" or "Extremely Satisfied," how hard would you fight to keep it (assuming someone is trying to take it away)? Share your answers with a small group. Be sure to discuss details—what exactly is not satisfying or extremely satisfying about your education?

Discussion Questions

1. When it comes to education, what are the factors that could contribute to gender inequality (in other words, educating boys before girls, not allowing women to attend university or punishing women for pursuing education)?

2. In areas that are plagued by poverty, education is still failing children. Even after years of studying, many children may not be able to read, write or solve basic mathematics problems. Why do you think this happens? What could be done to support children in impoverished areas of the world?

3. In 2017, a Japanese high school student in Fukuoka violently kicked his teacher multiple times because the teacher refused to return a tablet that the student was using to watch movies instead of study. (The news article and video can be seen at https://japantoday.com/category/national/japanese-high-school-student-repeatedly-kicks-his-teacher-while-class-is-in-session.)

Screenshot taken from video of incident.

This is not the only instance of violence between teachers and students. What do you think is happening to education? Are teachers losing classroom management skills or do students feel like they can do what they want with no worries of repercussions? What are the core problems, and are solutions on the horizon or is the situation going to get worse? What are classrooms like in your home country?

Speaking Strategies: Casual Speech versus Formal Speech

"Hey, what's up?"

"How are you doing today?"

Most people can probably identify which question above is the casual one. However, with the popularity of social media sites and blogs, casual speech is becoming more and more acceptable in formal settings. Even politicians and company CEOs have opted for a more casual tone in order to connect with the "average" customer or voter.

It is important, therefore, to understand the different levels of not only English, but any language you speak. Whether you are fluent or just learning "survival language" skills for travel, it is best to know when to say what to whom. Casual language has the power to not only make you *sound* fluent, but it can make also help you make friends with local people, learn new idiomatic expressions and slang words, and blend into the culture more easily.

This section is not meant to teach you informal speech. It is much too big of a topic to fit into this tiny section. Also, the chances are that you're already familiar with informal language from friends, television and movies, and YouTube videos. This section is meant to help you think about the casual words and expressions that you know, and when and where they might help you make friends...and when and where they might help you make enemies.

Casual language has a lot of benefits, but remember that it also has the power to offend your listener. Let's practice our casual speech skills (*not* offending skills)!

Speaking Activity Find one partner, and decide who will play the role of an average teenager and who will play the role of a high school teacher. Create a little script about not turning in homework, with the teenager using informal language and the teacher using formal language (Hint: If you need help with formal language, you could take a peek at the next unit). Next, act it out! After this role play is finished, switch roles! This time, the teacher is using casual speech and the student is the one who is using formal speech. Perform your play in front of the class, and then discuss the following: How did the conversations sound? Which part sounded stranger—a student trying to turn in an assignment using formal language or a teacher using casual language while not accepting it. What are some pros and cons of using casual speech in formal situations?

Unit Assignments

Topic: What would you teach?

Assignment: Group Presentations, Final Proposal, and Class Discussion; essay

In 2019, many universities across Japan extended classroom lesson times by 10 minutes (from 90-minute lessons to 100-minute lessons). Do you agree or disagree with this change? How would you structure a daily lesson? In other words, if you were a university professor, what would an average daily 100-minute lesson include? After everyone has presented their ideas, decide as a group which one is the best. Then, talk to your instructor about the proposal. Would she/he be willing to make the changes? Why or why not? Finally, discuss what changes you believe need to be made in current education systems.

UNIT 9: CULTURAL IDENTITY (FRANCE)

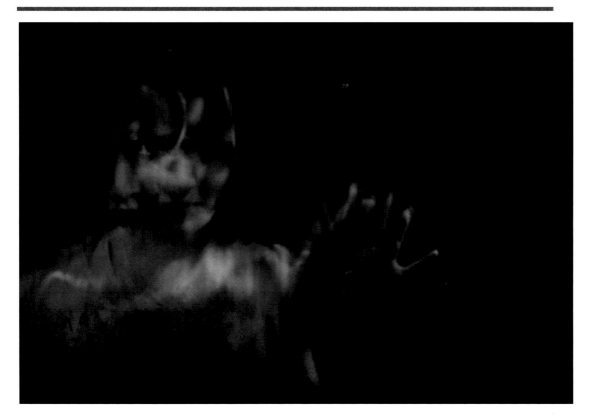

Vocabulary List

Check the meaning of the words and phrases below. Then use them in the activities in this unit.

1) identity

2) inclusion

3) acculturation

4) assimilation

5) integration

6) categories

7) ostracize

8) geopolitical

9) threat

10) depopulate

"Let me see your identification!"

If a police officer demanded from you for this piece of information, it would be very easy for most people to prove their identity. A driver license, student ID card or passport would probably meet this demand, as well as answer many other questions that the officer could have (e.g., birthdate). However,...

"What is your cultural identity?!"

This question would most likely be met with silence and confusion, and you would probably be arrested.

Cultural identity is not something easily explained. This is because our cultural identities are made up of many areas, such as language, ethnicity, race, family, religion, and gender. This is very similar to the "ME" chart we made in Unit 1!

There are many models that help to understand cultural identity, and while some of them differ, most of them agree that cultural identity is made up of many different social aspects. What language(s) you speak, the region of the world you were born and raised, religious or spiritual beliefs, traditions you follow, how much money your family has, where your family "ranks" in society, plus many more parts of one's life make up one's cultural identity. The crucial point you must consider is that cultural identity is not static! It changes and evolves with a person's experiences, travels, relationships, and jobs.

For example, a Japanese child who was born and raised in Tokyo, but suddenly moves to Australia at the age of 9 and lives there for the next ten years, will go through a cultural identity crisis as they determine which culture they identify with most. They may end up choosing to "be Australian," or decide to return to their roots and "be Japanese"—or, as many are doing now, they may choose to be a combination of both. While this type of combined cultural identity is common in Western countries, such as Canada and England, the concept is relatively new to monocultural countries like Japan and South Korea.

Activity It's time to explore your home country's cultural identity! What are some important parts that make someone a part of that culture? In other words, if you are American, what makes you "American"? For some, being patriotic is a big part of what it means to be American. For others, being American means loving baseball. Come up with four important aspects of your home country's culture, and then write your thoughts on why it's important.

Country: _____

Cultural Aspect	Why is it important to your culture?

Once you are finished with your chart, explain each cultural aspect to a partner or small group. Are there any parts that you agree or disagree with?

France

Say the word "France" to anyone walking down any street in the world, and the same images will probably come to mind: Paris, Eiffel Tower, Arc of Triumph, the Champs Elysees, baguettes, wine, cheese, berets, accordions, and romance. A phrase that probably no one would think of is *cultural identity*, but France is actually a very important country to examine regarding traditional cultural identity and the ever-changing definition of what it means to be French.

With the rise in immigration and refugee populations moving into Western European countries, France, like many countries in the European Union, have become an American-style "Melting Pot." In spite of all the benefits of having multiple cultures in one country, there are some groups that believe accepting non-French people into France is slowly destroying their culture. This idea is very interesting to consider because it is essentially a "protectionist" perspective that they have taken. In other words, their cultural identity—the core of their very existence—is being threatened through outside influences.

A perfect example of this is the story of José Bové, a French sheep farmer who, with some supporters, literally dismantled a McDonalds that was being built in his hometown (Northcutt, 2003). Instead of being labeled a racist or a nationalist, Bové was praised as a national hero for protecting his beloved France (and his French identity) from the effects of commercialism and globalization. In addition, with the rise in crime and terrorist attacks, 57% of French people surveyed state there are too many immigrants in France, and that their presence is "causing their country to change in ways they don't like" (The Local/AFP, 2016). When asked what the main cause for concern was, many respondents claimed it was the immigrants' inability (or lack of desire) to integrate into French society (ibid.).

This issue is a global "hot topic," and many governments and its citizens are fighting against immigration, open borders, and its country accepting more refugees. Are these fears grounded in reality, or is this fearmongering (the act of causing fear among a large group or community) from local leaders and politicians? There are no right or wrong answers, but this issue is relevant for almost every country in the world because it poses a vital question that requires an answer.

Discussion Questions

1. How tolerant is your home country of foreigners?
2. Are claims to cultural identity overly protected? In other words, if a person that is from one culture, but identifies as another culture, should this claimed identity be respected and For example, if a non-Japanese

person "feels" Japanese," and they do their best to live as a Japanese person and integrate into Japanese society—becoming a permanent resident, marrying a Japanese person, having children, working, paying taxes, and contributing to the economy and a pension plan—should that person be able to call themselves Japanese even if they don't have Japanese citizenship? (Any nationality can fit into this prompt for the sake of discussion!)

3. Recently there have been strong arguments against accepting immigrants and refugees. Describe some of these arguments, and discuss whether they are valid. (For this topic, the unit on religion (Unit 7) and education (Unit 8) can be used to give you some ideas!)

Speaking Strategies: Formal Speech versus Casual Speech

In the previous unit, we looked at casual speech, which can include jargon, idiomatic expressions, slang, and even offensive language ("curse words"). Casual speech is an important part of any language, and can give the speaker a sense of fluency that may lead to better understanding of the culture and closer friendships.

That being said, formal speech, is by far the best way to speak a language for several reasons. The most important, though, is that formal speech almost always well received by the listeners. 99% of conversations spoken with formal speech, which includes polite, respectful language, will be taken in positive ways. Whether you're talking to a teacher, a police officer, a fast-food restaurant employee or a stranger, formal speech should always be used.

One concern regarding formal speech has to do with its opposition: casual speech. Many people are choosing to spend several hours a day watching television or movies, or using their smartphones to chat, play games, watch YouTube or Netflix. A growing concern is that people are forgetting how to communicate properly. Some are choosing to withdraw from society completely by spending all day in their rooms on their cell phones, while others make attempts to engage in face-to-face communicate by repeating online jargon like "lol" (笑) at the end of a sentence:

This is not only happening in English-speaking countries. In Japan, for example, there are multiple levels of language, ranging from casual speech to *teineigo* (polite speech) to *keigo* (or honorific speech), and they are an extremely important part of the culture because they show respect for the listener. Young people have increasingly been unprepared for situations which call for respectful language, and usually study or are trained before interviews or jobs.

There's a way to get back on track by learning a few simple phrases that can be used in a variety of situations, and they always exude politeness and respect. "Please," Thank you," "You're welcome," "Excuse me," and "I'm sorry" should be your go-to phrases every single day. Let's look at some other examples of polite speech that will save your interview, presentation, conversation, and even your life:

Formal Expressions	Example	Create your own sentence
May I have...?	May I have more time to answer?	
Could I see...?	Could I have more time to answer?	
Please	May I have more time to answer, please?	
I'm hoping to	I'm hoping to have more time to answer.	
Is it possible to	Is it possible to have more time to answer?	
Let me know if...	Let me know if I can have more time to answer.	
To be honest, ...	To be honest, I need more time to answer.	

Lastly, while there are more phrases and plenty of rules to follow when speaking and writing formally, one very common point should be focused on here. When using informal speech, it is common to use contracted auxiliary verbs:

Informal: **It's** running smoothly.   vs.   Formal: It **is** running smoothly.

Informal: **She's** left the office.   vs.   Formal: She **has** left the office.

Learn these rules and phrases, and use them as often as possible. The critical message here is this: If you're not sure of which to use, defer to formal speech.

You will almost never offend anyone, and will more than likely make your listeners feel respected and appreciated.

Speaking Activity Practice your polite speech skills with a partner! Recreate the scenario from the previous unit, and see how the conversation would go if both the student and the teacher were using polite speech. After you've acted it out and discussed it, switch the scripts, and have the student and teacher talking to each other using the worst casual speech you know (nothing violent or degrading). After both skits are finished, discuss them with the class.

Unit Assignment

Topic: World's Most Polite Robbery

Assignment: Round-table discussion, reflection paper.

Watch the video titled "World's Most Polite Robbery" on YouTube (URL: https://www.youtube.com/watch?time_continue=84&v=45mgOuoVN4E), and notice the language that is being used during the robbery.

Screenshot taken from https://www.youtube.com/watch?time_continue=84&v=45mgOuoVN4E

How did you feel hearing the criminal explain his situation? Did you feel sympathetic to his problems? How did the cashier respond to the man? What do you think the man's punishment should be (the thief was caught two days later)? Should his sentence be more lenient because he was polite and rational about his reasons for robbing the store? Present your opinions and ideas to the class.

UNIT 10: FOOD AND EATING HABITS (AUSTRALIA)

Vocabulary List

Check the meaning of the words and phrases below. Then use them in the activities in this unit.

1) healthy

2) nutrition

3) fat

4) diet

5) carbohydrate

6) aborigine

7) cuisine

8) fast-food culture

9) vegetarian / vegan

10) survival

Food is all around us. We need it for survival. Food gives us energy, helps us maintain our lives, and helps us grow. It is a natural instinct to search for food when one is hungry, and people have been known to lie, cheat, steal, and even kill for food. The more humans evolve, the more food evolves, and we find new ways to grow, prepare, and present food to the hungry masses.

Whether you are a meat eater or a vegetarian (or vegan), food has the power to be undeniably delicious and beautiful. Ethnic cuisine can be found all over the world, and interest in a new culture is often started in a visit to a new ethnic restaurant. Chefs also travel to other countries to either study the local dishes or open up their own restaurant serving traditional foods from their culture. This global movement of culinary knowledge has led to "fusion" restaurants—restaurants that serve dishes that are a combination of foreign and local foods.

McDonald's has become a child favorite all over the world.

Activity What traditional foods are popular in your home country? What foreign foods have become popular? Are any foreign dishes commonly eaten during special times or events? For example, during Japanese *matsuri* (festivals), Middle Eastern kebabs (sliced meat stuffed into a pita bread) are common street foods that are sold in food stands. Write about popular foods in your home country (three traditional, three from other countries, and three during special times or events), and then share with a partner or small group!

Home Country: _____

Traditional food and dishes	Popular food from other countries	Popular food during special times/events
1)	1)	1)
2)	2)	2)
3)	3)	3)

In spite of all this beauty and creativity, food also has a negative side. What began as a necessity for survival became a fight for customers and profits. Science entered the food industry, and soon processed meats and artificial flavors flooded supermarket aisles and restaurant menus. Quality family time spent during meals turned into eating ready-made meals or fast food as quickly as possible while each person stares at their smartphone screen.

Obesity and other health issues related to food choices has also spread across the world, and rather than promote healthy eating and life choices, some people choose to continue eating unhealthy foods while embracing movements like body positivity and "plus-size" models. (For more information on Body Positivity, go to https://www.psychologytoday.com/us/blog/the-truth-about-exercise-addiction/201608/what-does-body-positivity-actually-mean.) On the other end of the spectrum are fad diets, such as the Keto Diet, body (or "fat") shaming, and eating disorders. Let's not forget the millions of people who are malnourished and starving because a shortage of food in their areas.

In short, food has become a complicated mess, ... but at least it provides a moment of happiness.

Australia

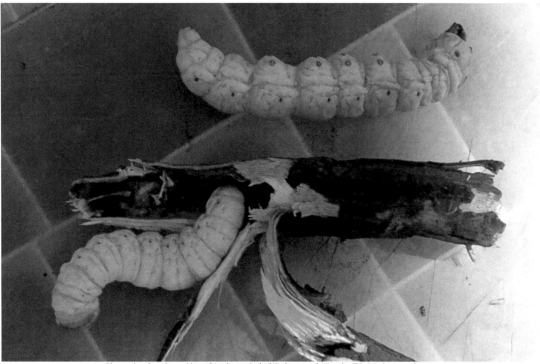

From 1984 to 1990, Paul Hogan, known across the world as Crocodile Dundee, looked into the camera and, with a dashing smile, invited us to Australia, promising to "slip an extra shrimp on the barbie for you." Since that time, Australia has yet to shake the image of shrimp being grilled on a barbeque, and it is this image that most people conjure up when asked about food in Australia.

However, there are two very interesting sides to our discussion of food in Australia. The first side covers the people commonly associated with the country of Australia—the "Aussies" as they are colloquially known. Although on the surface there may seem to be similarities with the British, they are quite different, especially when it comes to food. Australians have a wide variety of food products that were created and produced there, and many of these products are exported to and enjoyed by other countries.

One of the most famous Australian products is Vegemite. Black, tart, salty, and

uniquely Australian, this spread made from yeast extract is loved by Australian children and adults, and is eaten in a variety of ways, but most commonly on buttered toast. Other popular Australian products include Weet-Bix, a high-fiber cereal bar, and Tim Tam, a sweet treat made with two biscuits separated with chocolate cream and completed covered in a layer of chocolate.

Regarding dishes, the national dish of Australia is roast lamb or meat pie, depending on who you ask (responses seem to differ online, with one source stating that Australia doesn't even *have* a national dish). They also are known to eat crocodile and kangaroo meat, chiko rolls (inspired by Chinese spring rolls or egg rolls), ANZAC (Australia and New Zealand Army Corps) biscuits, and "snag" (i.e., sausage). While this is not an exhaustive list, these dishes and products are meant to paint a general picture of food and eating habits in Australia.

The second side of our discussion on Australian food and eating habits relates to the Aboriginal Australians. Aboriginal Australians were the first inhabitants of Australia, and have a unique culture that dates back centuries. The Aboriginal Australian males were generally the hunters (mainly of large animals), and the females were the gatherers (of plants and insects). Many of their ancestors' hunting and eating habits have been passed down to recent generations, and include scouring the land for food that many Westernized cultures would find revolting.

Take for instance the *witchetty grub* (pictured at the top of page 75). The witchetty grub is a large, white moth larva that eats wood. Although not the most appetizing food, they are high in protein and have helped the Aboriginal Australians survive. If you are able to, watch the video from the BBC (2008) titled "Aboriginal Witchetty Grubs & Honey Ants - Ray Mears Extreme Survival") (URL: https://www.youtube.com/watch?v=SJlO0aifJxA). Also seen in the video are Aboriginal women searching for certain ants in order to suck a sweet liquid from their abdomens.

The purpose of this section is not to disgust you, but intrigue you by opening your eyes to other cultures' eating preferences. They may be different, but humans share one common goal when it comes to food—survival and enjoyment. Because of this, all food should try to be viewed and understood from an open-minded, culturally respectful point of view. Remember that there is always something *you* eat that is very strange to people in another culture!

Discussion Questions

1. How important is food (and drink) in your culture? Is it embedded in certain cultural activities (e.g., bounenkai [忘年会] and shinnenkai [新年会] in Japan)?

2. What foods are tied to holidays (e.g., turkey during Thanksgiving in America) and religious activities (e.g., bread and wine or grape juice during Christian Communion)?

3. Should people stop eating food that is becoming scarce, endangered or taboo (e.g., whale, dolphin, dog, etc.)?

Speaking Strategies: Presentation Slide Tips, Part 1

Long gone are the days of carrying around a bulky easel pad and plastic box full of different colored markers for presentations. Replacing the easel pad was the white board-on-wheels, but the box of markers was still needed. Then, in 1987, a breakthrough program was created that would change the face of presentations forever: Microsoft PowerPoint. Now available for both Windows and Mac, PowerPoint has become "the most widely used application for creating a computer-based presentation or slide show" (Powerpoint, n.d.).

Since 1987, PowerPoint has gone through many changes, and other presentation programs were later introduced. Whether you use PowerPoint, Keynote, Prezi or any other program that makes presentations or slide shows, these tips will help you make a clear, easy-to-follow presentation that will focus attention on you and the message you're trying to deliver.

Point #1: Each slide should have a main header (or title). The header is usually a larger font than the rest of the text in the slide, and tells your audience exactly what the slide is about.

Point #2: Below the main header should be a few main points that you will discuss. These could be separated by numbers or bullet points. It is imperative that you avoid complete sentences! You want your audience to glance at the slide, pick up the main information, and then return their gaze to you as you explain each point in detail.

Point #3: Everyone loves pictures; however, the amateur presenter *overuses* photographs, often using multiple pictures instead of simple words to explain his or her main points. Choose your photographs wisely, and generally stay away from "cute" photographs that will draw attention away from your message.

Point #4: Adding to the confusion are animations. When the amateur presenter discovers animations—tools that can make words and photographs enter into, exit or disappear from a slide—he or she usually overuses them. The end result is chaos. *Everything* moves, shakes, disappears, flies in, and changes colors and sizes, making the audience nauseous and confused.

Point #5: Using charts and graphs, such as pie charts and bar graphs, to explain numbers, statistics or trends is a powerful tool, and often legitimizes presentations by highlighting research that supports the presenter's main message.

Point #6: Like photographs, use cartoons and other animated pictures sparingly, if at all. Hearts, unicorns, and anime characters are all cute, but they usually do not belong in academic and professional presentations (unless your presentation is on one of those topics, of course). More than likely, these cute animations will take away from your message and derail the audience.

Point #7: Use a standard presentation design. There are ways to use your own photographs or designs, but the designs that are available in programs like PowerPoint are generally all well used by professionals around the world. Try to find one that fits your topic and speaking style, and avoid choosing one that is difficult to focus on or that makes the words difficult to read.

Please note that these guidelines are for the slides only, and do not follow any kind of pattern or structure! In the following units, presentation structure will be discussed.

Unit Assignment

Topic: You eat what?!

Assignment: Presentation (with PowerPoint), Food Fair, journal entry, reflection paper

Reflect on what foods are eaten in your culture or by an ethnic group living in your home country. What are the staple foods? What food could be viewed as strange or interesting? What do poor people eat compared to what rich people eat? Conduct some research on the food (its history, ingredients, nutritional value, cultural significance, etc.), and present this information to your class.

If you are able to obtain some samples of food, check with your instructor to see if it's ok to bring some to class for people to try. If enough people bring different foods from their culture, you can have a Food Festival!

After the presentations (or Food Festival) are complete, write a quick journal entry (300-500 words) on how everything tasted (or looked, if you didn't eat anything), and what you learned from the different presentations. How did the food compare to what you're used to in your home country?

UNIT 11: CLOTHING AND FASHION (CHINA)

Vocabulary List

Check the meaning of the words and phrases below. Then use them in the activities in this unit.

1) trend

2) feminine

3) masculine

4) petite

5) plus-size

6) haute couture

7) prêt-à-porter (or Ready-to-wear clothing)

8) footwear

9) costume

10) dandy

A long, long time ago, one of the first humans emerges from his cave, and looks around. He notices that, while he slept, an amazing transformation has occurred. The brown dirt, grey rocks, and green trees and bushes were no longer their usual colors, but instead were covered with a strange white substance. Everything sparkled as the morning sun continued to rise. He takes a step out from his cave and curiously picks up some of the white powder. His feet sink into the newly formed white ground. Suddenly, he realized something so profound that it was to change the course of human civilization forever:

"It's freakin'[2] cooooooooooooooooold!"

So maybe this description isn't historically accurate, but at some point, the first humans came to the stark realization that they could no longer survive the harsh elements of this earth walking around naked. Researchers have narrowed down when humans began wearing clothes—around 170,000 years ago—but before that time, they note, "Our ancestors were likely running around nude and relatively hairless for quite some time then" until it became too cold for comfort (Viegas, 2011).

Since that time, humans have found many ways to stay warm and covered, mostly by using animal skins, as well as grass and other types of foliage. However, what was once considered a means for survival became one of the most significant determiners of a cultural group. The way one dressed signified the clan or tribe he or she belonged to, and this was important for many reasons. Let's consider some of those reasons now!

Activity Choose one group of people clothing from your home country with a unique style of clothing. You could choose teenagers, housewives (or stay-at-home moms), rap or hip-hop artists, Japanese salaryman, etc. Describe how they typically dress. Start from their footwear and move up, or from their head (hair/hat) and move down. Your description can also include things like hairstyle, jewelry, skin tone (e.g., tanned skin), tattoos, and so on. After you have finished describing how they typically dress, explain why you think they chose to dress that way.

---

[2] freaking (often spelled or pronounced "freakin'" to express casual speech): A word used to emphasize a situation, usually stressing surprise, anger, or annoyance at something or someone.

My home country:

_____

The Group I Chose:

_____

Description of How They Typically Dress:

_____

_____

_____

_____

_____

_____

_____

_____

_____

Why I think they choose to dress that way:

_____

_____

_____

_____

_____

_____

_____

_____

_____

_____

After you've written down your description and ideas, share with a partner or small group. Finally, have a class discussion and share some of your groups most interesting descriptions and thoughts!

Now let's return to our topic.

As everyone knows, fashion has now become a way to express individuality, the work they do, the school they attend, and even the street gang to which they belong. What we wear speaks volumes about who we are as a people, and every item, if you really think about it, has some cultural significance (note: Look back to Unit 1's discussion on people as cultural beings!). Fashion can be a source of praise (when one is wearing the latest fashion or an expensive brand name item), or a source of bullying (when one isn't wearing the latest fashion or is wearing cheap clothes that aren't "cool").

One of the most amazing aspects of fashion is that it has, at times, transcended concepts like gender, blurring the lines between masculine and feminine, and this is coming from both the haute couture (high-end fashion designer clothing) to prêt-à-porter fashion that is available in every street mall across the globe. Another amazing feat is that fashion has the ability to transcend language. For example, you don't need to speak Chinese to appreciate the beauty and innovation behind some of the fashion creations that come from China and Chinese designers, and this applies to other countries that speak different languages and have different cultures and fashion than yours.

China

One cannot discuss fashion without delving into the history of a country, and China has one of the oldest and richest. Fashion in China has a long, rich, and fascinating history. Because fashion is such a visual art, it would be best to actually see the various transitions and changes that Chinese fashion has undergone. While this seems like a near impossible task, one person—N. Duong (2013)—has managed to create a beautiful pictorial showing some of the various changes women's fashion went through during certain periods of China's history.

There are a few things to consider when looking at clothing and the development of fashion in a country. The first is the materials that were available to make the clothing; the second is the utilitarian aspect of the clothing produced (in other words, clothing that is designed to be practical rather than eye-catching fashion statements); the third is the influence on clothing design (influences can be areas within the country, like clothes worn in rural areas, climate change, war, foreign fashion influences, and so on.

 Apparently, there are four main types of traditional clothing worn by Chinese: the Hanfu (Han clothing), the Zhongshan suit (also known in foreign countries as the Mao suit), the Tang suit, which is in reference to the style of the jacket rather than the entire ensemble, and the cheongsam (*qipao*), which evolved from the Manchu women's long gown (Fercility, 2019).

Take a look at the poster on the next page that highlights some of China's fashion styles during different periods (Duong, 2013).[3]

Activity After reviewing the poster, respond to the following questions, and then share your answers with a partner or small group.

What are your initial thoughts on the clothing?

_____

_____

_____

_____

What influences do you believe caused the changes in fashion? Remember that influences can be areas within the country (e.g., rural style), climate change, war, foreign styles, etc.

_____

_____

_____

_____

Comment on the color of the dresses, the hairstyles, the accessories, and patterns of the fabric, the footwear. Can you see any outside influences in some styles?

_____

_____

_____

---

[3] (Note: To look more closely at the details of each drawing, N. Duong's (2013) complete poster can be viewed online at https://ninchanese.com/wp-content/uploads/sites/3/2013/06/Full_Chinese_fashion_timeline.jpg. Please note that the website and email address printed on the poster were not functioning at the time this textbook was published.

FASHION TIMELINE OF CHINESE CLOTHING

Fig. 1: **221 BCE–220 AD**
Qin to Han dynasties
1 piece garment is the main
formal wear for women

Fig. 2: **220–420 AD**
Wei and Jin dynasties
clothing is mainly large and loose

Fig. 3: **420–589 AD**
Northern dynasty

Fig. 4: **220–589 AD**
Wei, Jin, Southern and
Northern dynasties

Fig. 5: **420–589 AD**
Southern and Northern dynasties

Fig. 6: **581–618 AD**
Sui dynasty

Fig. 7: **618–907 AD**
Tang dynasty
Clothing is modeled after Sui

Fig. 8: **618–907 AD**
Tang dynasty
most open to foreign influence;
also influenced many other nations

Fig. 9: **618–907 AD**
Mid-Late Tang dynasty
Women's clothing become
more loose

Fig. 10: **960–1279 AD**
Song dynasty
Foot-binding begins to be
practiced by aristocrats' women

Fig. 11: **1271–1368 AD**
Yuan dynasty
China falls under Mongol rule

Fig. 12: **1368–1644 AD**
Ming dynasty
restoration of native role,
Yuan customs are abolished

Fig. 13: **1368–1644 AD**
Ming dynasty

Fig. 14: **1368–1644 AD**
Ming dynasty

Fig. 15: **1644–1911 AD**
Qing dynasty
China is conquered
by the Manchurians

Fig. 16: **1644–1911 AD**
Qing dynasty
The Manchurians attempt
several bans on foot-binding
but are unsuccessful

Fig. 17: **1911–1920s AD**
1927: Natural Breast Movement;
Native attempts on banning
foot-binding remain unsuccessful

Fig. 18: **1911–1920s AD**
Cheongsam: original dress from
the Manchurians, adopted by
the Chinese in the 1920s

Fig. 19: **1930s–1940s AD**
Dress is further westernized,
tailored to flatter body shape
1949: Footbinding is eradicated

Fig. 20: **1940s–1960s AD**
The cheongsam survives
as everyday wear until
the late 1960s

Fig. 21: **21st century**
Modern Era

The final topic to be discussed actually is connected to a holiday that was discussed earlier in this textbook: Halloween. While Halloween has long been connected to the walking dead, evil spirits, haunted houses, and horror movies, a recent trend has revelers dressing up as real people and, in many cases, as people from different cultures.

Some of these "cultural costumes" have been deemed inappropriate and even racist. One example is "blackface," or painting one's skin to look like an African American. This phenomenon is not limited to The United States and other countries where the majority are Caucasian. In 2017, the popular Japanese New Year's Eve show 笑ってはいけない (Waratte ha ikenai) dressed up one of the comedians as Eddie Murphy's character in Beverly Hills Cop, but took the costume further by painting his skin brown.

Screenshot taken from 笑ってはいけないシリーズ (Waratte ha Ikenai series), New Year's Eve 2017

This was seen as hilarious comedy in Japan, but many people from other countries voiced their concern and objection to the use of blackface. Besides blackface, other "cultural costumes" still exist, and are very popular during the Halloween season. Some cultural costumes include Japanese "geisha girls" and ninja, Arabs, Native American Indians, and Mexican "hombres" (men).

Photos taken from https://www.purecostumes.com

Dressing up as "Chinese people" is also an extremely popular choice for Halloween:

Photos taken from https://www.purecostumes.com

These costumes are essentially caricatures based on cultural and ethnic stereotypes. Many agree that these costumes are tongue-in-cheek (ironic or not serious) and therefore harmless fun; however, some argue that "cultural costumes" support and further strengthen false beliefs, stereotypes, and even racism. In other words, they are not culturally appropriate.

Cultural appropriation is becoming a topic of great importance in today's multicultural society. Cultural appropriation, according to the Cambridge Dictionary, means "the act of taking or using things from a culture that is not yours, especially without showing that you understand or respect this culture." However, as shown above, there are times when acts are viewed with contempt and outrage (e.g., blackface in Japan) while other acts are lauded (blackface in the 2008 comedy movie *Tropic Thunder*). It is another difficult topic that deserves more of our attention and discussion.

Discussion Questions

1. Why does clothing change over time? Why can't fashion and clothing choices remain the same? Use examples from your home country, history, movies, fashion magazines, and/or knowledge of another culture to explain possible answers.

2. When fashion changes, so cultures lose something in the process? In other words, is a part of that culture forgotten if, as we saw with the Chinese, traditional clothes are replaced by modern Westernized fashion?

3. Are "cultural costumes," like the Halloween costumes shown above, appropriate to wear? In other words, is being "a Chinese person" for Halloween harmless fun or does wearing this type of costume perpetuate racial and ethnic stereotypes?

Speaking Strategies: Presentation Structure, Part I

Some would agree that the beginning of anything—a poem, a song, a play, a new job, a friendship, a conversation, a meal, a lesson—is the most important part, as it sets up what is to come. The same can be said for a presentation, a classroom discussion or a formal debate. How you begin will prepare your audience for what they are about to see and hear. A sound structure to your presentation, discussion or debate will help you create a persuasive and memorable message for your audience. Let's look at one way we can accomplish this!

Like any academic essay, there is always a beginning, a middle, and an end. The beginning to an academic essay is called the Introductory Paragraph, and we are going to take aspects from these types of paragraph to structure our presentations, discussions, and debates. Take a look at this flow chart for a speech, presentation or opening remarks for a debate:

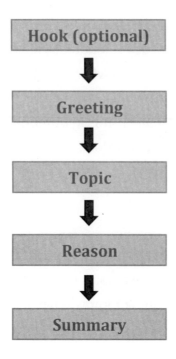

The **first step** is optional, but strongly recommended. A "hook" is a way to grab your audience's attention, and this can be accomplished in a number of ways. One way is to ask a question—usually a rhetorical question, or a question that doesn't require an answer from the audience. For example, if your topic is Halloween Cultural Costumes, you could begin by asking, "Would you ever consider dressing up as a Chinese person for Halloween?" If you're using PowerPoint or a similar program, another way to do this is to show a photograph, chart, graph, map, etc., and ask a question. Going back to our example, you could show one of the costumes above and ask, "Would you ever consider wearing one of these costumes for Halloween?" Your questions don't need an answer, so don't wait for one! Don't pause for too long after you ask your question, and simply continue with your presentation. A third way to grab your audience's attention is by making a bold statement: "Halloween and racism. These two words may not seem connected, but they are." There are many more ways to create a hook for your presentation or speech, so be creative the next time you have to give one!

The **second step** is the basic greeting. Saying "good morning/afternoon," "or even a simple, "Hello" will create a feeling of warmth and connection between the speaker (you) and the audience. Don't forget this key point!

The **third step** is introducing your topic. This can be done in a number of ways, but try this standard phrase: "Today, I'm going to talk about _____ (your topic)." It's a very simple, yet very effective way to let the audience know what the focus of your presentation or speech will be.

Although the third step seems to be the most important, it can be argued that the **fourth step** is, as it establishes the reason why you're presenting this topic in the first place. Why are you talking about Halloween costumes? More importantly, why should the audience care about Halloween costumes? There needs to be a solid rationale as to why you're discussing this topic, otherwise the audience won't become invested in what you have to say. In short, you need to give them a reason to care about what your topic. Usually, but not always, the rationale is your opinion on the topic. Look at these two examples:

"I want you to stop buying cultural costumes for Halloween because I think they are racist!"

vs.

"Cultural costumes for Halloween may unknowingly offend people from the cultures that are being represented, so it is important to discuss the cultural significance of these costumes so that better choices can be made."

What is the difference between the two? While it is clear that the second one is more detailed, there is one small difference that makes a huge impact on your message. Notice that "I" is missing from the second example. This is critical because, while both examples are opinions, the first one sounds too *subjective* (*based on the speaker's feelings or opinions*). The second example, while still an opinion, sounds more *objective* (not influenced by the speaker's feelings or opinions). This is an important point to remember when giving presentations, speeches, and debates!

The **fifth step** is the summary. This is the part that lets the audience know what your main points will be. This step will be covered in more detail in the next unit, but for now, just remember this line: "I'm going to talk about three points."

Speaking Activity Follow the flow chart above, and complete the introduction for a presentation you're giving on Chinese fashion.

Hook (optional):

Greeting:

Topic:

"From the Chinese Timeline of Fashion, the best outfit is from _____

because it is _____

_____."

Reason:

"It is important to know this information because _____

_____."

Summary:

"I will talk about three points."

After you complete the boxes above, take turns presenting your introduction to the class. Give each other advice on strong points and areas that could use improvement.

Unit Assignment

Topic: Uniforms for All

Assignment: Debate, Group Presentation, or Academic Essay

Present, discuss, debate or write about the following topic: All schools at every level (from day care to graduate school) should make it mandatory for students to wear uniforms. Come up with three reasons why this is a good idea. If this is a class debate, one group will come up with points that support this idea, and the other team will come up with negative points. Find research, political opinions, possible dangers, etc., and use them to support your position! At the end of the presentations or debates, the instructor will decide which argument was more persuasive.

UNIT 12: SPORTS AND RECREATION (VARIOUS COUNTRIES IN AFRICA)

Vocabulary List

Check the meaning of the words and phrases below. Then use them in the activities in this unit.

1) recreation

2) athletics

3) Africa

4) wrestling

5) occupy (a country)

6) attribute

7) compete

8) championship

9) league

10) uniform

Sports

Many topics covered in these units bound certain groups together. Sharing the same ethnicity, nationality, or religion, for example, intertwines peoples' lives in a way that is unique in this world. Other topics, such as education, draw like-minded individuals to each other, and those individuals create a community of support and trust even though they may not share some of the aspects mentioned above. As we'll learn in a moment, sports have the power to create "armies" of people loyal to one team, and those groups show their passion in various ways. Usually this passion manifests itself in positive ways, but it can also create chaos, violence, and damage cities.

Sports are such a powerful force that countries have adopted a national sport (formally, but sometimes informally). According to one source, cricket is the national sport in India (and many other countries); sumo wrestling is the national sport of Japan (although baseball is more popular); archery is the national sport of Mongolia; volleyball is the national sport of Sri Lanka; and baseball is the national sport of the United States (although many will argue that it's American football) (Wood, 2015). These are just some examples of the wide variety of sports that are played and adored across the world.

Activity What is your home country's national sport (formal and/or informal)? Why did it become so popular? Have you tried to play the sport before? What sports have you played, and want to try? After you write your answers below, explain your choices to a partner.

My home country: _____

National Sport(s)	
Most Popular Sports (besides the National Sport)	
Sports I've played	
Sports I want to try	

It is difficult to cover every country and every national and popular sport, so let's just look at one country in more detail. Here is list of popular sports in Japan, from 2005, 2011, 2013, 2016 and 2017:

Favorite professional sport	2005	2011	2013	2016	2017
Baseball (Nippon Professional Baseball)	51.7%	45.1%	48.4%	42.8%	45.2%
Sumo	17.1%	15.1%	15.8%	21.8%	27.3%
Association football (J. League)	22.8%	28.9%	36.0%	26.2%	25.0%
Tennis (Japan Open)	N/A	N/A	N/A	20.6%	21.7%
Do not care about sports	24.4%	22.0%	18.9%	24.0%	18.2%
Golf (Japan Golf Tour)	16.9%	19.9%	16.0%	13.4%	13.7%
Boxing	7.8%	7.7%	7.8%	9.8%	9.2%
basketball (B.League)	N/A	N/A	N/A	N/A	6.0%
Motor racing	6.2%	7.7%	7.0%	7.0%	5.2%
Puroresu	4.2%	3.1%	3.5%	4.7%	3.8%
Others	8.0%	5.7%	7.8%	3.7%	7.8%

Chart taken from https://en.wikipedia.org/wiki/Sport_in_Japan

Most countries have their own traditional sports, as well as sports that were imported from other countries. This importing of sports can often be attributed to colonialism, or political and military occupation. For example, traditional sports in Japan include *kyudo* (Japanese archery, which also includes "mounted archery"—archery performed while riding a horse), kendo, aikido, and judo. However, from the chart above, it is interesting to note that baseball—a sport imported from America—is the most popular sport in Japan even though it is not considered the national sport. Interestingly enough, the national sport, sumo wrestling, has been steadily climbing in popularity, while soccer ("Association football") has been slowly declining.

A sport's popularity depends on many factors, including national and international championships, high-profile games, such as the Olympics, and the rise of sports icons. If you're not sure about how popular a sport is, consider this: Who is the most popular sports figure in your home country? The most popular sports figure usually tells a lot about the importance of a certain sport in a country.

Recreation

Boredom can strike at any moment. One minute you're working hard on a class assignment, and the next minute you're fighting a strong urge to get up and go do something you love to do. Those activities that are done for enjoyment, amusement, and fun are categorized as *recreation*. Recreation can include physical activities that are not generally organized sports, such as hiking, bicycling, surfing, and working out. They can also include games, such as board games or puzzles like the Rubik's Cube. Again, if you're doing something to win a medal or recognition, that activity ceases to be recreation and turns into either a job (e.g., professional ice skater) or a professional pursuit (e.g., sponsored skateboarder). Recreation, like sports, is extremely important for cultural groups, and usually tells a lot about what is considered fun in a given area.

Activity What types of recreation are most popular in your home country? Which do you enjoy doing? How long have you done them? Have you thought about turning your recreational activity into a profession? Write your thoughts below and then share them with a partner or small group.

Various Countries in Africa

There are 54 countries in Africa, and each country is filled with a long history, fascinating beliefs and traditions, and, of course, a variety of sports and recreation! It is impossible to discuss all 54 countries in this textbook, so only a few will be covered. However, you are encouraged to research some countries to discover what traditional and modern sports are played, and what recreational activities are done.

There is one sport that has spread across almost every country in Africa—football (known as soccer in every country except the United States). It should come as no surprise that many African countries struggle with resources, so playing a sport that requires a minimal amount of equipment makes perfect sense. Many African countries, such as Nigeria, Senegal, and Tunisia, have been recognized as having strong football clubs, and because of these teams, football has grown in popularity.

Although needing a bit more equipment than football, rugby has also become quite popular in African countries, and South Africa, Kenya, and Ghana has helped increase the number of professional teams in Africa. Other popular sports including marathon running and other athletics, cricket, and basketball.

Traditional sports are rich in tradition and history. The most ancient traditional sport seems to be wrestling, which is practiced in many villages across Africa.

Photo taken from https://www.africa.com/8-most-popular-sports-in-africa/

Wrestling has been a part of African villages for a long, long time, but there are other sports that have ancient roots in Africa, as well.

Another sport called *Ta kurt om el mahag* is considered by some to be the sport that inspired baseball in the West. A much more dangerous (and sometimes deadly) sport is called "stick fighting," which has two fighters basically beating each other with sticks. This sport is so bloody and violent that South Africa has banned it; however, proponents argue that the sport "encourages cultural expression and requires skill, discipline and a firm physique" (Hungryng, 2017). Other sports include *bavika* (like a Western rodeo show with dangerous bulls), and donkey racing.

This section is not a critique of traditional and modern sports in African countries, but rather an attempt to show how diverse sports can be in one continent.

Trying to summarize recreation in a continent is, again, an impossible task. However, one interesting recreational game that will give an amazing insight into the history of Africa is called *mancala*. If possible, watch the video titled "How to play mancala" (URL" https://www.youtube.com/watch?v=-A-djjimCcM), or search that phrase online for a quick demonstration.

Screenshot taken from https://www.youtube.com/watch?v=-A-djjimCcM

Mancala holds the distinction of being one of the oldest, if not *the* oldest, board game in human history, and involves basic pieces—stones or seeds and a wooden board. The rules are a bit complicated to explain in this unit, but the goal is basically to capture all of your opponent's stones using a variety of moves.

It is amazing to look at a game like mancala and imagine the different ways in which humans have found enjoyment. Mancala and many other games and activities have been a source of recreational enjoyment for centuries, and we should learn more about other culture's sports and recreational activities in order to better understand each other. Who would have thought that a simple game could be so meaningful to our lives!

Discussion Questions

1. What do you think about South Africa banning stick fighting? Do you agree or disagree that a country should tell people how they can spend their free time?

2. Many countries are losing interest in traditional sports and recreational games. Should countries do more to establish professional sports teams and championship games in order to attract more attention to them, or should some sports (such as stick fighting or donkey racing) be forgotten as the culture changes?

3. What are some popular board games from your home country? Explain their significance to your culture. For example, Monopoly is one of the most popular board games in America, but few know the history behind the creator's motivations: "[Elizabeth Magie Phillips] created two sets of rules for her game: an anti-monopolist set in which all were rewarded when wealth was created, and a monopolist set in which the goal was to create monopolies and crush opponents" (Pilon, 2015).

Speaking Strategies: Presentation Structure, Part II

In the previous unit, the introduction of a presentation or speech was covered. In this unit, we will continue with a sound structure of a presentation (speech or academic written assignment). From the introduction, you can naturally transition into the main part of your presentation, which consists of your main points. In academic writing, this main section is often referred to as the "body" of the essay. These main points contain two parts: explaining the main point and providing support.

The key to the first part is the explanation, and this largely falls on your shoulders. Giving clear, accurate, and engaging explanations is a skill that many public speakers constantly work on. Try to aim for 4-5 sentences that provide a clear picture of your main point. Many speakers make the mistake of rushing to the supporting sentences, thinking that the audience will not believe their argument until they see a graph, chart or statistic that provides undeniable proof. Take your time explaining as much as you need to in order to paint that vivid picture for your audience.

The second part is the support, and this can take many forms. Statistics, graphs, charts, and pictures can assist speakers and writers with strengthening their main point. When writing academic papers or giving academic presentations, it is important to consider the sources of your information. Technology has made it extremely easy to find information, but be sure that the website you get your information from is a legitimate source. Don't rely too much on Wikipedia, as anyone can change the content on wiki pages!

As you can see from the flowchart below, the final part of the process is transitioning or changing smoothly into your next part. This can be easily accomplished by remembering this simple phrase: "Now that I have talked about _____ (First Main Point), I'm going to talk about _____ (Second Main Point)."

Introduce Main Point

Provide an explanation

Give examples and statistics to support your main point

Transition into your next Main Point

This flow chart is not a new concept, and has been used in academic writing for many years. The great part of this type of structure is that it can be applied to writing, but also speeches and presentations.

Speaking Activity Choose a game that you played when you were a child, and describe the first part of the game (not the entire game) using the format above. For example, most people know the game "Paper, Scissors, Rock" (じゃんけん in Japanese), so try to explain the first part of the game (e.g., using hands to play, the different positions, and what beats what/what loses to what). Be sure to explain the part, provide an example to illustrate the part, and then transition into your next part.

Unit Assignment

Topic: Your Move!

Assignment: Group Presentation / Demonstration, Poster Presentation or Project Plan

Work with a partner or small group to create a new recreation game or sport! Be creative as possible, and use your combined imagination to create a new game that incorporates both traditional and modern elements. Anything is possible (for example, using hover boards to fly above the ground)! Draw pictures to illustrate certain parts (e.g., team uniforms, equipment, etc.). After you have finished, explain your new sport or game to the class! Be sure to explain how traditional and modern elements have been incorporated.

UNIT 13: POPULAR CULTURE (UNITED STATES)

Vocabulary List

Check the meaning of the words and phrases below. Then use them in the activities in this unit.

1) pop culture

2) consumer

3) melting pot

4) global

5) commercialism

6) emigrate

7) norms

8) engrained

9) adaptation

10) icon

When people think of "pop culture," they usually think of famous people, products or objects from a certain country that have cemented themselves into that country's history that they become synonymous with that culture. This definition is only partially true, though. Pop culture also includes practices, beliefs, and even activities that become so engrained in the culture that they come to represent that culture. Because the concept of pop culture is so broad, icons can be found in "movies, music, television shows, newspapers, satellite broadcasts, fast food and clothing, among other entertainment and consumer goods" (Levin Institute, 2017).

Every pop culture icon, whether it be a thing, a place, a person, a belief or an activity, can be placed into a certain pop culture category:

- **entertainment** (movies, music, TV)
- **sports**
- **news** (as in people/places in news)
- **politics**
- **fashion/clothes**
- **technology** (West, 2013)

If you're having difficult coming up with a pop culture icon, just think about the most popular people, places, activities, movies, television shows in your home country. Whatever you're thinking of right now is most likely a pop culture icon!

Pop Culture Wallpaper created by ConfessionOnMDNA (2019)

Activity Thinking of your home country, try to come up with at least one example of a pop culture person, place or item for each of the categories. Remember that as long as the person or object is important to your culture, it can be considered part of pop culture. There are really no wrong answers!

My home country: _____

Category	Pop Culture Object, Place or Person	Brief Description (Why is it/he/she popular?)
Entertainment		
Sports		
News		
Politics		
Fashion/clothing		
Technology		
Your idea: _____		

While pop cultural icons are a source of entertainment for many, there are some who don't share as much enthusiasm for them. Pop culture is viewed by some as being a front for commercialism, with big business profiting off of the poor and working class through the constant promotion of their products. With a daily bombardment of television commercials, billboards, magazine covers, consumers eventually succumb to the idea that the product or person is, in fact, a pop culture icon, and spend money to support them. Other critics warn that with the rise of celebrities who are "famous for being famous," icons who were once talented and charismatic, like Marilyn Monroe and Elvis Presley, are being usurped by Kim Kardashian, Nicki Minaj, and others who do little more than sell their sex appeal and controversial views to the masses. (For those interested in exploring these critiques more, check out the science fiction comedy movie titled *Idiocracy* by Mike Judge (2006)!)

It should be understood that this unit presents just one way to define and categorize pop culture, as well as some critiques of pop culture. Like the definition of *culture*, there are many ways to view, define, analyze, and perceive pop culture and pop culture icons, and there is no "right" or "wrong" way—just different perspectives that are usually influenced by our own culture, experiences, preferences, and opinions (Strinati, 2004). Feel free to agree or disagree with anything presented here! As mentioned many times in the textbook, the goal is to spark critical thinking and discussion.

American Pop Culture

Photo of Charlie Girard's White Mountain Puzzles *Pop Culture Collage* - 1000 Piece Jigsaw Puzzle

"Images of America are so pervasive in this global village that it is almost as if instead of the world immigrating to America, America has emigrated to the world, allowing people to aspire to be Americans even in distant countries."

-Former Canadian Prime Minister Kim Campbell

This quote from former Canadian Prime Minister Kim Campbell is telling of how powerful American pop culture has been on the entire world. The most popular American pop culture icons have withstood the test of time, meaning many years have passed and they are still popular, well known, and often mentioned in news, television shows, movies, and advertisements.

Good examples of pop culture icons that continue to be representative of the American culture are:

- McDonalds,
- Coke,
- Mickey Mouse,
- Hollywood,
- Marilyn Monroe,
- Baseball,
- Rock and Roll,
- Elvis,
- the Empire State Building, and
- the American Dream.

When you read this list, you most likely pictured in your mind these places, people, things, and ideas. What is even more amazing than this is that most people's brains, upon hearing any one of these items, would immediately connect them to America. American pop culture has dominated the world for years, and many images have no doubt caused many people in various countries to share the same dream of moving to America and living out the "American dream."

Interestingly enough, because of America's "melting pot," other countries' pop culture icons have crept into America and blended into American pop culture. Popular examples of this are Godzilla, sushi, Ultraman, kimono, Hello Kitty, and samurai imported from Japan.

Cover of Mark Shilling's book *The Encyclopedia of Japanese Pop Culture* (1997)

What impact has your home country had on other countries? No matter where you are from, there is something—even a small part—of your culture that has had an effect on people living in different parts of the world. Pop culture is an incredibly powerful tool for communicating cultural ideas, norms, and values, and can transcend language, cultural identity, gender, and even national borders. An openness to reflect on these icons in popular culture, whether positive or negative, as well as the other cultural aspects that have been presented throughout this textbook, is a great springboard to our final discussion on Global Critical Thinking (GCT).

Discussion Questions

1. Is culture becoming "dumbed down" by commercialism and new waves of pop culture icons (e.g., iPhones, Billie Eilish, video-sharing social networking services, like TikTok and Snapchat, etc.)? What good can come from pop culture spreading to other countries? What bad could come from it?

2. Is American pop culture having a negative or a positive effect on the rest of the world? Do you think countries should start rejecting pop culture icons that are damaging cultural norms and traditions?

3. Discuss your favorite pop culture icons from your home country, as well as from foreign countries. Try to think of pop culture icons that come

from both Eastern countries and Western countries. What is appealing about them? Do you think pop culture will change tremendously in the twenty years? How?

Speaking Strategies: Presentation Structure, Part III

Finally, we come to the *conclusion*—the final statement given to an audience to solidify the message of the presentation, speech, or essay. You have laid out your introduction and have explained and supported your main points. The good news is that the hard work is done! All that remains is to summarize your main points, thank your audience, and then check if anyone has any questions. (Note: These final two steps can be omitted if you are writing an essay). Let's break down these three final steps!

Step 1: Summarize your Main Points

You have already explained in detail what your main points are, why they are important, and supported this with an example, a chart, a graph, or some kind of photograph or image that illustrates the connection between your point and researched or documented data. The final step is to take all this information and summarize it in 1-2 sentences. The easiest way to do this is to say, "In conclusion," and then simply restate your main "thesis" sentence and briefly remind your audience of its importance or significance to your entire message. The flow will sound something like this:

"In conclusion, I discussed _____ (*main theme of your presentation or speech*). First, I discussed _____ (*First Main Point*). This is important because _____ (*state the significance and support*). Second, I discussed _____ (Second Main Point). This is important because _____ (state the significance and support). Finally, I discussed _____ (*Third Main Point*). This is important because _____ (*state the significance and support*)."

What you will say for the significance and support parts will change based on what you actually focused on in your presentation. The script above is just to give you an idea of how the flow of your conclusion should be, but be flexible and open to changing it to fit your theme and speaking style.

Step 2: Thanking your Audience

This is one of the easiest parts of your presentation or speech, but you would be surprised how often amateur speakers mess it up. It is important to read your audience first before delivering your thank you, and we can do this by asking ourselves some critical questions:

- Did my presentation go over the time limit?
- Do I need to clarify a missed point?
- Do I need to apologize for something?
- Are audience members visibly tired or in need of a bathroom break?
- Do they look confused? In other words, did I not explain my main points effectively?
- Was my presentation serious or light-hearted and fun?
- Did I connect with the audience?

Many more questions can be asked before saying thank you, but, based on the answer to those questions, choose the best "thank you" for your situation. A simple "Thank you" with a genuine smile will never be taken poorly, whereas a quick casual "Thanks" with an exhausted or exasperated look may rub people the wrong way. The best thank you is a sincere one, so remember that your audience sat through your presentation or speech, so a heartfelt sign of appreciation is required.

Step 3: Q & A

Some speakers will switch Steps 2 and 3, choosing to ask the audience for questions, and then thanking them. However, two thank yous are better than one! Thank them (Step 2), wait for your applause to end (sometimes there won't be applause, so don't let that alarm you), and then simply say, "Do you have any questions?"

Here's a valuable speaking tip: Try to learn your audience member's names. If there are 300 members of your audience, this is impossible; however, if it were a small group of 10-15 members, this is a manageable amount of names to remember. If there are questions from certain members whose names you remember, calling on them *by name* will have a powerful effect on them, and they will remember you as a caring, focused, and engaged speaker.

If you don't remember their name, a simple way to address them is first saying, "OK, miss/sir, you have a question?" Before they begin speaking, fit in, "I'm sorry, what's your name again? Takashi? OK, Takashi, what's your question?"

After you respond to their question, finish with, "Thank you for your question, Takashi." This will give the appearance that you remembered their name!

Speaking Activity Use the information in the chart below ("Becoming a Superhero") to make a conclusion. The best practice is fun practice, so practice and have fun with your conclusion!

Topic: Becoming a Superhero

Main Point #	Main Point	Support
1	*Create a name*	According to a survey, 9 out of 10 superheroes choose their names by asking family members or friends for advice.
2	*Buy a superhero outfit*	According to The Newspaper, 75% of superheroes buy their costumes from Aeon Department Stores.
3	*Acquiring a superpower*	Your local space alien has superpowers for sale, but they are very expensive!

Remember to use the script that was provided above, but feel free to adjust it in order to fit the main points' significance and support. Take turns practicing the conclusion, and don't forget to give each other advice on ways to improve!

Unit Assignment

Topic: Get That Cultural Icon Out of Here!

Assignment: Debate, Roundtable Discussion, or Academic Essay

A new country is being formed, and the government is deciding whether to ban pop culture icons from the country in order to protect their culture and promote their own products (movies, candy, art, actors, sodas, etc.). Decide whether you are for or against this idea, and hold a debate on the good points and bad points of allowing other countries' pop culture into their own. Make sure you support your ideas and opinions with support, and remember to follow the debate structure, as well as other speaking points learned throughout the textbook. Either the teacher or one student (or both) can be chosen as moderator.

UNIT 14: GLOBAL CRITICAL THINKING

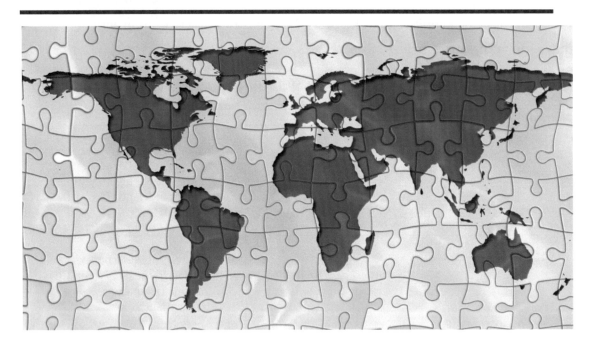

Vocabulary List

Check the meaning of the words and phrases below. Then use them in the activities in this unit.

1) cultural intelligence

2) critical thinking

3) globalization

4) xenophobia

5) diversity

6) emotional intelligence

7) cultural sensitivity

8) intolerance

9) static

10) enlightened

In 2001, an important film was made. This film was to change the way people all across the globe would think about culture, cultural differences, cultural adaptation, rejection, and acceptance, and an enlightened sense of cultural awareness and understanding that would shatter one's static worldview and create a new and improved worldview—a Global Critical Thinker (Velasco, 2018).

That film was...Pixar Animation Studio's *Monsters, Inc.* (distributed by Walt Disney Pictures).

OK, so maybe the film didn't impact the field of cultural studies, but it is going to get the attention it deserves in this textbook, as the characters and storyline depict the perfect setting of culture clashes, cultural rejection (and maybe even a type of racism) based on cultural differences, and final growth and acceptance.

If you haven't seen the movie, the basic story is this: Our human world exists, but in another "world" there exists the monster world. This monster world is run on energy produced from children's screams, which are "captured" when monsters enter the human world through closet doors and scare children. (This idea comes from the "monster in my closet" that was commonly feared and cried over by millions of children). The children are scared, they scream, their screams are collected, and the monster world uses those collected screams to produce electricity, gas for cars, etc. It is important to note that the monsters believe that children are dangerous, and that even one touch form a child could lead to death.

The two main characters in the film are Sully and Mike. Sully mistakenly allows a child (later named Boo by Sully) to enter the monster world, and attempts to hide the child while trying to return her to the human world. His best friend Mike tries his best to get rid of the child, and becomes angry at Sully's growing warmth and care for Boo. Mike does his best to protect himself, his best friend Sully, their jobs at Monsters, Inc., and their friendship, but each one falls apart with every moment spent with Boo.

This culminates when Sully finally makes the difficult decision to abandon Mike in order to save Boo.

Now let's get into our analysis of this animation, and how it connects to becoming a Global Critical Thinker.

The description above sets up our first cultural analysis: the monsters as one culture and the human children as another. The monsters don't hate the children so much as they fear them, and this fear is based on false beliefs—stereotypes—that are perpetuated by those who may not have ever interacted with any children, but continue to spread the presumption. The monsters, in essence, are conditioned from a very young age to fear the unknown culture.

Mike, although caring and kind-hearted, represents the side that rejects what is different, ambiguous, and unknown. Hofstede, Hofstede & Minkov (2010) call this *Uncertainty Avoidance*. In essence, Mike's own cultural identity is being threatened by this new cultural being (Boo), and he is doing his best to protect his identity and the identity of his best friend.

Throughout most of the movie, Mike even refers to the child as "It," thus reducing her identity to a thing rather than a living creature that deserves respect. The main antagonist in the film—a chameleon-type monster named Randall—attempts to exploit human children by using them as a resource for energy, which, through his methods of extracting screams, would kill them. He disregards their human lives as being less significant than monsters, and therefore can make use of and dispose of them if it serves the interests of their dominant culture.

The child, in contrast, accepts the monsters as equal to humans, and, although she fears Randall, she understands that not all monsters are "Randalls" (i.e., meant to be feared). She enters this new country (the monster world), and views it with a wide-eyed curiosity that many people experience when traveling to a foreign destination. She does not feel out of place, but instead feels as though she belongs—as if she has a right to be there, even if her presence is only temporary.

Sully begins the movie holding the same fear and avoidance that the others monsters have of humans, but eventually opens up to this new "culture." (Research Hofstede, Hofstede & Minkov's (2010) concept of *Uncertainty Avoidance* for more information on this fear of the unknown or ambiguous.)

The turning point is when he is forced to confront his own "scary" behavior that he once was proud of:

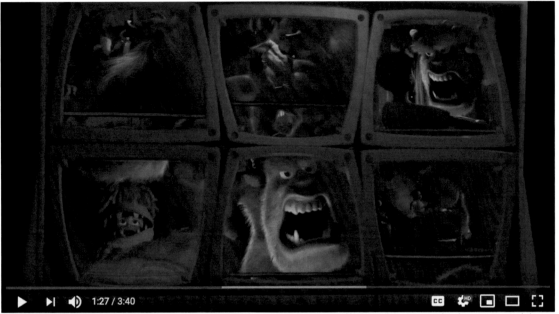

...and realizes that *he* is the monster to be feared, not Boo.

It is only by this harsh realization that Sully finally accepts his own false beliefs and fears, and adapts his behavior to accommodate both cultures, not just his own.

While comparing the difficulty in accepting and adapting to a culture different than our own to a popular animation film might not seem serious, the message is ultimately the same: Cultures are different, and our behavior may seem "normal" to us, but it can easily be viewed as "abnormal" to other cultural groups. Getting past these cultural obstacles is where our journey toward Global Critical Thinking begins!

Activity What are some stereotypes of your own culture? What stereotypes do individuals from your cultural group hold (and pass on to younger generations) about different cultural groups? Try to come up with three stereotypes for three different cultural groups. Don't be afraid to write examples down! We are not here to judge one another, but to learn from and grow with each other, and opening up about and discussing stereotypes is one way.

Stereotypes about my home country:

_____

_____

_____

_____

Stereotypes about other countries:

1)_____

_____

2)_____

_____

3)_____

_____

The term "critical thinking" has been a buzzword in education for many years, but it was only recently that the term "Global Critical Thinking" was introduced into the field. Velasco (2019) explains both critical thinking and Global Critical Thinking:

> Critical thinking has been a key phrase in education for years, producing a variety of definitions. Lai (2011) provides one clear definition of critical thinking: "Critical thinking includes the component skills of analyzing arguments, making inferences using inductive or deductive reasoning, judging or evaluating, and making decisions or solving problems" (p. 2). With globalization entering education jargon, "Global Critical Thinking" (GCT) is a

more of an appropriate phrase for today's classroom goals. GCT combines both critical thinking skills and cultural understanding (in other words, one's own culture, as well as other cultures around the world). . . . One way to accomplish GCT is to broaden students' perspectives and understanding of the world around them. (p. 291)

It is often said that the world is growing smaller due to globalization, technology, and travel, so it is time for the citizens of the world to move away from ethnocentric beliefs and adopt a more open, respectful, and genuinely interested perspective of those who may be different from us. There are many parts of the world that are dangerous, and, yes, there are some people out there who are trying to take advantage and hurt others, but this should not stop us from developing into Global Critical Thinkers.

The overarching goal is not to make the entire world one country where everyone is the same. Differences should be acknowledged, understood (to the best of our ability), respected, and celebrated. There will always be those who fight against this perspective, but with every discussion, we move one step closer to the goal.

Discussion Questions

1. Countries that are mainly monocultural, like Japan, have been known to not accept those who are different from them. However, with issues such as declining birthrate and an aging society, they are left with little choice but to accept more foreigners into their country. What are some ways countries with high levels of Uncertainty Avoidance (Hofstede, Hofstede & Minkov, 2010) can begin to be more accepting of the unknown?
2. Generally speaking, stereotypes are bad for fostering tolerance and positive intercultural relationships. Can you think of any good that comes from stereotypes?
3. In this unit, Monsters, Inc. was used to show how different cultures may come to fear one another. Think of another story, movie, television show, news report, etc., that could illustrate different cultures coming to understand and accept each other, and share it with a partner or small group (i.e., tell the story as if you were a storyteller).

Speaking Strategies: The Outline and Preparation

Every good speech, presentation or essay needs a plan, and this section will cover the basics of a good outline, as well as preparation tips for any upcoming speaking project (including the upcoming Final Assignment in Unit 14).

 There are hundreds of outline formats available in books and online resources, so it is recommended to find one that flows with your style of research and speaking. You will find an outline structure below that combines the last two units, making a complete outline for a presentation or speech.

I.   Introduction
    a. Hook
    b. Greeting
    c. Topic
    d. Reason
    e. Summary (of Main Points in Body)

II.   Body
    a. First Main Point
        i. Explain
        ii. Support
    b. Second Main Point
        i. Explain
        ii. Support
    c. Third Main Point
        i. Explain
        ii. Support

III. Conclusion
    a. Summarize your Main Points
    b. Thank your audience
    c. Q & A

Again, this is just one way you can organize your presentation or speech, so use this outline format if you find it helpful or find a structure that best fits your topic and speaking style. For the upcoming Final Assignment in Unit 15, try to use this outline structure and see how it works for you.

Unit Assignment

Topic: Preparing for the Final Assignment

Assignment: Presentation (Research and Outline)

Your instructor should have assigned you a theme or topic and a country to focus on. Using this information, research your theme in relation to the country, and decide on a focus. Use a cluster map (similar to the "ME" chart you created in Unit 1) to create ideas.

After you have decided on a topic, it's time to conduct some research! There is a lot of information online, but be careful of which sites you get research from, as some websites act as propaganda tools for political parties and/or agendas. The best way to conduct research is still in a library, so visit your school's library and see what books and journals they have on your topic. All of these topics are well-researched and published, so it will not be difficult to find information no matter your topic or country.

After you have collected enough material to support your focused idea, it's time to create an outline. Use the format above to create a rough outline for your presentation. An **Outline Form** is provided on the next page. (Tip: It may be a good idea to make a few copies of the Outline Form so that you can brainstorm ideas and not have to worry about making mistakes or changes in the textbook.) When you have finished, bring your outline to class and get feedback from a partner and your instructor!

After you have revised your outline, it's time to begin creating your script and PowerPoint. This is the final step of your journey to become a Global Critical Thinker, so, when you're ready, move on to the last unit—Unit 15.

Outline Form

I.   Introduction

    a. Hook (optional, but recommended)

_____

_____

_____

_____

    b. Greeting

_____

_____

_____

_____

    c. Topic

_____

_____

_____

_____

    d. Reason

_____

_____

_____

_____

    e. Summary (of Main Points in Body)

_____

_____

_____

_____

II.   Body

    a. First Main Point

_____

_____

_____

_____

        i. Explain

_____

_____

_____

_____

_____

ii. Support

_____

_____

_____

_____

_____

b. Second Main Point

_____

_____

_____

_____

i. Explain

_____

_____

_____

_____

_____

ii. Support

_____

_____

_____

_____

_____

c. Third Main Point

_____

_____

_____

_____

i. Explain

_____

_____

_____

_____

_____

ii. Support

_____

_____

_____

_____

_____

III.   Conclusion

_____

_____

_____

_____

_____

_____

a. Summarize your Main Points

_____

_____

_____

_____

_____

_____

b. Thank your audience

_____

_____

c. Q & A

_____

_____

Feedback Notes:

UNIT 15: FINAL ASSIGNMENT

This unit is actually not like the other units in this textbook, but is rather the recommended final assignment for your class. This assignment combines everything learned in this textbook, and provides an opportunity to conduct further research into the assigned cultural area and theme.

Look at the chart below. You can see that there is a different country connected to a different theme. There are three ways the chart can be used:

1) This chart can be used as-is, and students can be randomly selected for each row;
2) students can choose their own row based on their interest; or
3) the teacher can randomly mix the countries and themes, and randomly assign students to each one.

Either way, you're going to research a country and a theme. The beauty of this assignment is that you may focus on any area within that theme. For example, if your chosen theme is "Education in Pakistan," then you can choose to explain the different types of education available to children and young adults, or you can choose to explain the difficulties women have obtaining an education, and use Malala as support for your presentation.

Here is the chart that has been pre-made for this textbook:

Student Name	Country	Topic/Theme
	Japan	cultural identity (e.g., bi-racial or ハーフ)
	India	ethnicity (e.g., ethnic group conflicts)
	France	religion (e.g., religious group conflicts)
	USA	traditions
	Philippines	gender
	England	pop culture
	Brazil	gender
	Italy	beliefs
	Germany	education
	Thailand	ethnicity (e.g., issues with racism)
	Iraq	clothing/fashion
	Vietnam	religion
	(North or South) Korea	traditions
	Turkey	gender
	Nigeria	beliefs (e.g., superstitions and/or religious beliefs)
	Indonesia	sports/recreation
	Switzerland	politics
	Spain	ethnicity
	Canada	clothing/fashion

These topics were randomly generated, and some of them repeat. This is because there are many topics that can be discussed *within* these areas, Examples have been given for several themes, such as "ethnicity" "beliefs" to show the breadth of topics that can be taken from the general theme. Be sure to confirm what your final choice is with your instructor before beginning research.

The end result should be a 5-10-minute oral presentation (final time limits will be set by your instructor), using PowerPoint or another presentation program.

Be sure to incorporate several legitimate resources to support your research, ideas, and opinions, and don't forget the speaking and presentation skills you learned throughout the course.

Alternative assignments can be found on pages 141-144, so wait for your instructor to confirm which assignments will be used during the semester, and which will be used as a final project. Regardless of which assignment is used, the objectives remain the same: to expand your peers' knowledge of culture and society, thus adding to the learning that has already taken place throughout the semester using this textbook!

References

Asian Correspondent. (2019). 'The nail that sticks out gets hammered down': Bullying in Japan. Retrieved from https://asiancorrespondent.com/2012/07/the-nail-that-sticks-out-gets-hammered-down-bullying-in-japan/

Barrett, D. B., et al. (2001). World Christian Encyclopedia: A Comparative Survey of Churches and Religions in the Modern World. U.K.: Oxford University Press.

Blood, P. (1994). *Pakistan: A Country Study*. Washington: GPO for the Library of Congress. Text can be retrieved from http://countrystudies.us/pakistan/42.htm

Central Intelligence Agency. (2019). World Factbook: Russia. Retrieved from https://www.cia.gov/library/publications/the-world-factbook/geos/rs.html

culture. (n.d.). Definition. Cambridge English Dictionary. Retrieved from https://dictionary.cambridge.org/us/dictionary/english/culture

cultural appropriation (n.d.). Definition. Retrieved from https://dictionary.cambridge.org/us/dictionary/english/cultural-appropriation

Fercility. (2019). Traditional Chinese Clothes—Hanfu, Tang Suit, Qipao, and Zhongshan. Retrieved from https://www.chinahighlights.com/travelguide/traditional-chinese-clothes.htm

Hofstede, G. (2020). The 6 dimensions of national culture. Retrieved from https://www.hofstede-insights.com/models/national-culture/

Hofstede, G. (2020). Uncertainty Avoidance. Retrieved from http://clearlycultural.com/geert-hofstede-cultural-dimensions/uncertainty-avoidance-index/

Hofstede, G., Hofstede, G. J., and Minkov, M. (2010). *Cultures and Organizations: Software of the Mind*. New York: McGraw-Hill.

Hungryng. (2017). Top 7 African Traditional Sports. Retrieved from https://www.hungryng.com/african-traditional-sports/

Levin Institute. (2017). Pop Culture. Retrieved from http://www.globalization101.org/pop-culture/

Marchessault, J. K., and Larwin, K. H. (2013). Structured Read-Aloud In Middle School: The Potential Impact On Reading Achievement. *Contemporary Issues in Education Research*, 6(3). The Clute Institute.

Naviwala, N. (2017). What's Really Keeping Pakistan's Children Out of School? Retrieved from https://www.nytimes.com/2017/10/18/opinion/pakistan-education-schools.html

Nicoladis, E., Nagpal, J., Marentette, P., and Hauer, B. (2019). Gesture frequency is linked to story-telling style: evidence from bilinguals. *LANGUAGE AND COGNITION*, 10(4): 641 DOI: 10.1017/langcog.2018.25

Northcutt, W. (2003). Jose Bove vs. McDonald's: The Making of a National Hero in the French Anti-Globalization Movement. Retrieved from http://hdl.handle.net/2027/spo.0642292.0031.020

PBS. (2020). World Religion Maps. Retrieved from

https://www.pbslearningmedia.org/resource/sj14-soc-religmap/world-religions-map/

Pew Research Center. (2017). The Changing Global Religious Landscape. Retrieved from https://assets.pewresearch.org/wp-content/uploads/sites/11/2017/04/07092755/FULL-REPORT-WITH-APPENDIXES-A-AND-B-APRIL-3.pdf

Pilon, M. (2015). Monopoly's Inventor: The Progressive Who Didn't Pass 'Go.' Retrieved from https://www.nytimes.com/2015/02/15/business/behind-monopoly-an-inventor-who-didnt-pass-go.html

ConfessionOnMDNA. (2019). Pop Culture Icons Wallpaper. Retrieved from https://www.deviantart.com/confessiononmdna/art/Greatest-Pop-Culture-Icons-Wallapeper-550246812

Powerpoint. (n.d.) *THE FREE ON-LINE DICTIONARY OF COMPUTING.* (2003). Retrieved from https://encyclopedia2.thefreedictionary.com/Powerpoint

RT News. (2008). One million Muslims, one mosque. Retrieved from https://www.youtube.com/watch?v=xb0wmui7hTE

Sewell, P. (2013). Why Russia fails in ethnic conflict resolution. Retrieved from https://www.rbth.com/blogs/2013/08/19/why_russia_fails_in_ethnic_conflict_resolution_29007.html

Strinati, D. (2004). *An introduction to theories of popular culture.* U.K.: Routledge.

The Local/AFP. (2016). Majority in France against immigration. Retrieved from https://www.thelocal.fr/20160823/immigration-negative-for-france-majority-says

USAID. (2019). Pakistan: Education. Retrieved from https://www.usaid.gov/pakistan/education

Velasco, D. (2015). Evaluate, analyze, describe (EAD): Confronting underlying issues of racism and other prejudices for effective intercultural communication. *IAFOR Journal of Education, 3*(2), 82-93. Retrieved from http://iafor.org/iafor-journal-of-education-volume-3-issue-2-summer-2015/

Velasco, D. (2018). Incorporating TV commercials in university classes. JALT CUE Circular, Issue 7, November 2018, 9-11.

Velasco, D. (2019). Using TV Commercials to Promote Critical Thinking and Cultural Understanding. *PanSIG Journal 2018.* Tokyo, Japan: Japan Association for Language Teaching (JALT).

Viegas, J. (2011). Humans First Wore Clothing 170,000 Years Ago. Retrieved from https://www.seeker.com/humans-first-wore-clothing-170000-years-ago-1765156178.html

West, G. (2013). So, What Is Pop Culture, You Ask? Retrieved from http://mrpopculture.com/what-is-pop-culture

Woods, R. (2015). Lists of National Sports. Retrieved from https://www.topendsports.com/sport/national-sports.htm

World Atlas. (2020). Religious Demographics of Italy. Retrieved from https://www.worldatlas.com/articles/the-religious-demographics-of-italy.html

World Economic Forum. (2020). Global Gender Gap Report. Retrieved from https://www.weforum.org/reports/gender-gap-2020-report-100-years-pay-equality

Photographs and Images

Photographs and images are either referenced underneath the photographs in each unit or are listed here. Photographs from https://pixabay.com are free to use for commercial use with no attribution required.

Front Cover (Japan Osaka Night): https://pixabay.com/photos/japan-osaka-night-asia-landmark-2014616/

Page 6 (Human Observer): https://pixabay.com/photos/human-observer-exhibition-2944065/

Page 8 (Completed ME Chart): Copyright belongs to the author (D. Velasco, 2019)

Page 10 (Hardworking): https://pixabay.com/illustrations/stopwatch-hustle-and-hustle-hours-60204/

Page 15: (Urban People): https://pixabay.com/photos/urban-people-crowd-citizens-438393/

Page 22 (Japan Temple): https://pixabay.com/photos/japan-temple-tradition-japanese-2086585/

Page 28 (European Union Flags):https://pixabay.com/photos/blue-building-pattern-freedom-1283011/

Page 35 (Russian Dance): https://pixabay.com/photos/folklore-dance-russian-dance-3514259/

Page 33 (St. Petersburg, Russia): https://pixabay.com/photos/st-petersburg-russia-nonoj-petersburg-1034319/

Page 43 (Trans-Sexuality): https://pixabay.com/illustrations/trans-sexuality-transsexual-man-3554250/

Page 45 (Mind the Gap): https://pixabay.com/photos/railway-platform-mind-gap-1758208/

Page 51 (Retro Housewife): https://pixabay.com/illustrations/retro-housewife-vintage-collage-1254131/

Page 52 (Roundtable): http://www.clipartpanda.com/clipart_images/hands-on-shareholders-69860759

Page 53 (Stained Glass): https://pixabay.com/photos/stained-glass-spiral-circle-pattern-1181864/

Page 55 (World Religions pie chart): https://openclipart.org/download/253551/World-Religions-Percentages.svg

Page 55 (Distribution of World Religions): http://commons.wikimedia.org/wiki/File:Religion_distribution.png

Page 58 (Muslim Prayer): https://pixabay.com/photos/many-audience-people-group-muslim-3108666/

Page 61 (Child reading Bible): https://pixabay.com/photos/child-reading-bible-bed-african-945422/

Page 62 (Education): https://pixabay.com/photos/book-asia-children-boys-education-1822474/

Page 67 (Ice Cube Meme): http://www.quickmeme.com/meme/36hbrt

Page 69 (Identity): https://pixabay.com/photos/people-woman-identity-disorder-2559571/

Page 72 (Eiffel Tower): https://pixabay.com/photos/eiffel-tower-paris-city-history-1784212/

Page 74 (I dunno LOL): https://knowyourmeme.com/memes/i-dunno-lol-_o

Page 77 (Eating): https://pixabay.com/photos/hunger-hungry-eating-cookie-413685/

Page 78 (Child eating McDonald's): Copyright belongs to the author (D. Velasco, 2019)

Page 84 (Hamburgers): https://pixabay.com/photos/burger-fast-food-hamburger-731298/

Page 85 (Fashion): https://pixabay.com/photos/girl-student-asian-glasses-friends-1741925/

Page 98 (Sports): https://pixabay.com/photos/soccer-sport-red-play-ball-foot-434343/

Page 99 (Woman Running): https://pixabay.com/photos/woman-running-run-fitness-sports-1822459/

Page 102 (Africans Wrestling): https://www.africa.com/8-most-popular-sports-in-africa/

Page 107 (Pop Culture): https://pixabay.com/photos/graffiti-wall-graffiti-graffiti-art-1209761/

Page 117 (Earth Puzzle): https://pixabay.com/illustrations/continents-puzzle-world-earth-1219541/

Page 120 (Child's Drawing): Copyright belongs to the author (D. Velasco, 2019)

Page 129 (Library): https://pixabay.com/photos/books-library-room-school-study-2596809/

Page 149 (The Road): https://pixabay.com/photos/the-road-beams-path-forest-nature-815297/

Back Cover (Monk with Umbrella): https://pixabay.com/photos/umbrella-buddhism-monk-monastery-1807513/

Vocabulary Workbook

Unit 1
Match the vocabulary word on the left with the meaning on the right.

1. ____Culture

2. ____Society

3. ____Race

4. ____Ethnicity

5. ____Gender

6. ____Sexual Orientation

7. ____Socioeconomic Status

8. ____Identity

9. ____Profession

10. ____Descriptors

a. the division of humankind based on physical characteristics, ancestry, etc.

b. state of being male or female

c. a person's identity in relation to their sexual attractions

d. characteristics that make up who a person is

e. profession or career, usually earned after training or education

f. customs, traditions, arts, institutions, etc. of a people or group

g. something that describes or identifies a person, place, or thing

h. group that has the same national or social traditions

i. position in society based on money

j. a group or people living together and sharing customs, laws, etc.

Unit 2
Create your own sentence with each vocabulary word. Check your sentences with a partner.

1. knowledge:

2. belief:

3. custom:

4. tradition:

5. habit:

6. community:

7. region:

8. law:

9. organization:

10. ethnic group:

Unit 3

Use the words and phrases from Unit 3 to complete the sentences below. Practice with a partner!

1) In the U.S. and other Western countries, _____ is a celebrated idea.

2) Many European cities have both historic and _____ architecture.

3) _____ means that the group is more important than the individual.

4) Do you believe in a _____, or are you agnostic?

5) Taking off shoes before entering a home is the _____ in Japan.

6) Different cultures have different ideas of _____, or raising children.

7) My family was very traditional, so my mother's role was homemaker.

8) A _____ I've had since childhood is to "knock on wood" to stop bad luck.

9) _____ is important for people who believe in the spirit and soul.

10) In Japan, *osechi* is a _____ meal eaten on New Years Day.

Unit 4

Circle the synonyms (words that have the same or similar meaning) for each vocabulary word. There are TWO!

1) government   a. administration   b. laws   c. leadership

2) politics   a. president   b. affairs of state   c. diplomacy

3) vote   a. elect   b. poll   c. popular

4) legislation   a. presentation   b. law   c. rules

5) citizen   a. native   b. resident   c. a watch

6) economy   a. school subject   b. financial   c. wealth

7) conservative   a. traditionalist   b. right-wing   c. left-wing

8) liberal   a. progressive   b. right-wing   c. left-wing

9) democracy   a. elective gov't   b. dictatorship   c. republic

10) (political) party   a. gathering   b. group   c. affiliation

Unit 5

Match the vocabulary word on the left with the meaning on the right.

1) ____history   a. investigating sources to find an answer to a problem

2) ____ethnic group   b. a disagreement, argument or fight, usually between two groups

3) ____diverse   c. the number of people in a region or area

4) ____population   d. people who share the same cultural background or ancestry

5) ____(cultural/ethnic) minority   e. variety; different types of something

6) ____to get along (with)   f. to have a friendly relationship with someone

7) ____research   g. the study of past events

8) ____dialect   h. a relatively small group of people living within a larger group

9) ____artifact   i. any object made by humans

10) ____conflict   j. language that is special to a certain area

Unit 6

Create your own sentence with each vocabulary word. Check your sentences with a partner.

1) sex (in contrast to *gender*)

2) cultural

3) biological

4) LGBT(QIAPK)

5) gender gap

6) inequality

7) gender role

8) gender equal

9) attain

10) empowerment

Unit 7

Use the words and phrases from Unit 7 to complete the sentences below. Practice with a partner!

1) The religion of Muslims is _____.

2) _____ members sometimes have strange religious beliefs.

3) There are real dangers to religious fanaticism, or _____.

4) I don't believe or disbelieve in God, so I guess you can say I'm _____.

5) The largest religious belief in the world is _____.

6) A campaign to make a big change in religious beliefs is called a _____.

7) A system of faith and worship is called _____.

8) A _____ is a widely held but simplified view of a cultural or ethnic group.

9) My best friend isn't religious, but she definitely believes in _____.

10) What special _____ does your culture do to celebrate weddings?

Unit 8

Circle the antonyms (words that have a different meaning) for each vocabulary word. There is ONE answer!

1) institution   a. organization   b. association   c. ending

2) reform   a. maintain   b. preserve   c. change

3) literacy   a. ability to read   b. illiteracy   c. ability to write

4) diploma/degree   a. resume   b. certificate   c. credentials

5) disparity   a. imbalance   b. balance   c. discrepancy

6) urban   a. countryside   b. city   b. metropolitan

7) socioeconomic   a. money   b. finances   c. starvation

8) vocational school a. hotel   b. trade school   c. job training

9) academic   a. scholastic   b. scholarly   c. informal

10) disproportionate a. uneven   b. equal   c. unequal

Unit 9
Match the vocabulary word on the left with the meaning on the right

1) ____identity

2) ____inclusion

3) ____acculturation

4) ____assimilation

5) ____integration

6) ____categories

7) ____ostracize

8) ____geopolitical

9) ____threat

10) ____depopulate

a. a division or class or people or things

b. adapting to a new culture, but still holding on to some parts of the original culture

c. fully absorbing and becoming a part of a new culture

d. to reduce the population of one area

e. intent to inflict physical pain or other type of harm

f. to exclude someone from a group or society

g. characteristics that determine who or what a person or thing is

h. relating to politics that are influenced by areas or regions

i. combine two things so they become a whole

j. to become part of a whole (group, culture, etc.)

Unit 10
Create your own sentence with each vocabulary word. Check your sentences with a partner.

1) healthy:

2) nutrition:

3) fat (*n*):

4) diet:

5) carbohydrate:

6) aborigine:

7) cuisine:

8) fast-food culture:

9) vegetarian:

10) survival:

Unit 11

Use the words and phrases from Unit 11 to complete the sentences below. Practice with a partner!

1) Gucci and Versace are considered _____.

2) Every Halloween, a cultural _____ offends people.

3) These sunglasses are made for men, but they look very _____.

4) There are S, M, and L sizes, but I am so small that I need a _____ size.

5) Tomboys are females that are act very _____.

6) I don't like _____ or "off-the-rack" clothing because it's not original.

7) Shoes, boots, and sandals are all types of _____.

8) Did you see the new "body positive" _____ models in the magazine?

9) What is a current fashion _____ in men's clothing?

10) A man that is concerned with style and fashion is known as a _____.

Unit 12

Circle the synonyms (words that have the same or similar meaning) for each vocabulary word. There are TWO!

1) recreation	a. work	b. fun	c. leisure
2) athletics	a. sports	b. leisure	c. contests
3) Africa	a. a group of countries	b. people	c. a continent
4) wrestle	a. boxing	b. grapple	c. fight
5) occupy	a. controlling	b. fighting	c. taking over
6) attribute	a. connected to	b. taste	c. credit
7) compete	a. equality	b. try to win	c. challenge
8) championship	a. group of teams	b. contest	c. winner
9) league	a. collection of people	b. baseball	c. group of teams
10) uniform	a. clothing	b. outfits	c. hats

133

Unit 13
Match the vocabulary word on the left with the meaning on the right.

1) ____pop culture   a. relating to the entire world

2) ____consumer   b. people, places, and things that are popular in a country

3) ____melting pot   c. a person or thing that is an important symbol

4) ____global   d. a place that has many people from different cultures

5) ____commercialism   e. what is considered usually or common in a country or area

6) ____emigrate   f. changing to fit into a new culture or environment

7) ____norms   g. focus on making money by selling as many products as possible

8) ____engrained   h. a person who buys products

9) ____adaptation   i. to leave one's home country to live in another country

10) ____icon   j. to firmly establish in a person or culture

Unit 14
Create your own sentence with each vocabulary word. Check your sentences with a partner.

1) cultural intelligence

2) critical thinking

3) globalization

4) xenophobia

5) diversity

6) emotional intelligence

7) cultural sensitivity

8) intolerance

9) static

10) enlightened

Additional Assignments

The following assignments can be used in lieu of other units, as a midterm project, or as a final project (instead of the recommended final project in Unit 15). The time frame for these assignments is two classes (plus research and writing outside of class time), but this will also depend on class size, language ability, and other factors.

Note: **Activity 1**, **Activity 2**, and **Activity 3** are taken the article "Using TV Commercials to Promote Critical Thinking and Cultural Understanding (Velasco, 2019).

Activity 1

Unit: Unit 5: Race and Ethnicity

Topic: Racist or a Product of It's Time?

Time frame: Two classes (recommended)

Assignment: Role Play

First class: Access the video "Folgers Coffee Sexist 60s Ads, 2011" from YouTube (URL: https://www.youtube.com/watch?v=WMrRd6MYJP8). After viewing the video, students will be placed into groups of two or three, and develop one of the following tasks:

1) Recreate one of the coffee ads to reflect a more "modern" family.

2) Reenact one of the commercials, switching the genders.

3) Act out one of the commercials as it is presented.

Second class: Act out the role play in front of the entire class. After all the role plays have been acted out, discuss how you felt during the performance. Reflect on the coffee videos. Are they racist, or can they be viewed from a cultural lens from a previous time? In other words, would it be fair to judge something from the past with a modern point of view? Analyze the implications of such an action on society, relationships, intercultural communication, Global Critical Thinking, etc.

Activity 2

Unit: Unit 5: Race and Ethnicity

Topic: The Gentrification of Africa

Time frame: Two classes (recommended)

Assignment: Individual or Group Presentations

<u>First class</u>: View the video "Racist Chinese Laundry Detergent Ad Qiaobi (俏比) ad, 2016" (URL: https://www.youtube.com/watch?v=X27dvuBSyXE). After viewing the video, students will be placed into groups of three or four, and work on a 5-minute presentation on the commercial, as well as issues reflected in the commercial.

Some questions to be addressed in the presentation:

- Was the commercial racist, or simply cultural differences/ misunderstandings?
- What other issues came up in the commercial?
- How could this commercial reflect (either correctly or incorrectly) Chinese cultural values and beliefs?
- What did you learn from the experience?
- If you could reshoot the commercial, what changes would you make?

Students should be given poster board or large pieces of paper, markers (or have them use pens and pencils they have), and any optional materials to make the posters more interesting and colorful (e.g., old magazines).

<u>Second class</u>: Have students present their presentations to the class, and elicit feedback from the audience. After all the presentations are finished, have a class discussion on what can be learned from media that presents racist, sexist, and any discrimination or prejudice. How can we grow as Global Critical Thinkers after encountering such media?

Activity 3

Unit: Unit 6: Gender

Topic: Traditional and Modern Gender Roles

Time frame: Two classes (recommended)

Assignment: Evaluate, Analyze, Describe (E.A.D.) (Velasco, 2015)

<u>First class:</u> Access the video "Kool-Aid Kids in Japan 1960 commercial, 2013" from YouTube (URL: https://www.youtube.com/watch?v=WMrRd6MYJP8). After viewing the video, students will be placed into groups of two or three, and develop the following task:

Participants are shown the commercial twice. Have the students just watch the first viewing. For the second viewing, have them write information for the three categories (evaluate, analyze, and describe). Students are asked to:

- first evaluate how they feel about what is happening;
- next, analyze the situation—i.e., why it is happening; and
- describe the situation in the video in the simplest terms.

Give the students 15-20 minutes to write out their responses for each category. After they have finished, play the video once more, and then have them review what they wrote. If there is time, have the students discuss the three categories with a partner or small group.

<u>Second class:</u> Play the video again. Students can either share their findings to the class, or share them with a partner or small group. This can be followed by a group or class discussion. After the class discussion, have the students write an in-class journal/reflection paper/essay on what their experiences with the E.A.D. What did they learn from the activity, and how can this new knowledge and experience carry over into new intercultural situations?

Activity 4

Unit: Unit 6: Gender

Topic: Traditional and Modern Gender Roles

Time frame: Two classes (recommended)

Assignment: Discussion, Research Presentation (with PowerPoint or poster), or essay

First class: Make small groups, with three students in each group. Each group must choose one country. After the country is chosen, assign research roles for the following:

1. Men

2. Women

3. LGBT+ (or LGBTTTQQIAAQIA[4])

Have each student discuss information they know now (without researching).

Second class: Have students present the information that they gathered from researching (online or in a library) their part. What interesting facts, opinions, struggles, etc. did each student find? After the small group discussion, the group can present an overview of their chosen country's views on traditional and modern gender roles.

---

[4] This acronym is constantly evolving, so it is important to check which form is the most current at the time this assignment is being completed. A good list of definitions is available on many websites, including https://ok2bme.ca/resources/kids-teens/what-does-lgbtq-mean/. Please be careful of websites that promote discrimination of any kind or spread false beliefs about any group.

Disclaimer

Any website mentioned in this textbook is neither endorsed by nor connected to the author or the publisher. Information on websites change rapidly, and so the author and the publishers cannot and will not be held legally responsible for any of the content found on any website that is searched for and viewed while completing activities in or research for this textbook.

Instructors who choose to adopt this textbook are advised to check each website they plan to use in their lessons *before* asking students to view the site. Instructors may also choose to only show website content in class (either on a projector screen or printed out on handouts) to ensure the content being viewed is appropriate for their students and lessons, and issue a warning to the students about internet dangers. This is the preferred method of the author, and one that he has employed for every class he has taught.

Specific URLs for websites and online videos are only provided to give additional information on a topic. They are not mandatory parts of any unit. At the time of publication, the websites and videos were checked by the author to ensure they provided the information that they claim to give.

Any topic can be searched freely and safely online, and every person should always be careful of which websites they choose to view. It is important to remember that many websites offer personal opinions (often masked as facts), so any information found should be fact-checked. Aside from known facts or common knowledge, nothing should ever be considered 100% truthful, accurate and/or the final say on any matter.

Acknowledgements

I would like to thank the following professors for their valuable advice, insight, and support: Dr. Gregory Glasgow, Professor Donald Patterson, and Professor Stephan Johnson. A very special thank you to my mentors, Dr. Viviane de Castro Pecanha and Dr. Sandra Baca.

Also, a big thank you to my seminar students over the past five years. You kept asking me for a textbook to accompany my seminar classes, and, finally, here it is. This textbook could not have been possible without your passionate participation, humor, openness, and honest feedback about the course content.

Finally, the biggest and most important thank you goes to my family, who gave me enough time alone in my home office to complete this textbook. Without your love, patience, and support, none of my professional accomplishments would have been possible. This book is dedicated to you.

Comparative Culture and Society

2020年3月31日　　初版発行

著　者　　**ダニエル・ヴェラスコ**

定価（本体価格1,750円＋税）

発行所　　株式会社　三恵社
〒462-0056 愛知県名古屋市北区中丸町2-24-1
TEL:052(915)5211
FAX:052(915)5019
URL:http://www.sankeisha.com

ISBN978-4-86693-095-4 C3082 ¥1750E

ISBN978-4-86693-095-4
C3082 ¥1750E

定価（本体価格1,750円+税）

Comparative Culture and Society

by Daniel Velasco, PhD

This textbook contains fifteen (15) short units that give students opportunities to discuss, debate, present, and write about global topics and are paired with one country, so that each topic can be viewe perspective. Included in most units are:

- Vocabulary relevant to the theme being discussed
- Brief readings that provide basic information about
- Activities for individuals and small groups
- Discussion questions that stimulate open, respectful
- Speaking strategies to help students better express t
- Final projects that promote Global Critical Thinking (GCT) skills!

This textbook can be used as a main or supplemental classroom textbook, and is a great way to bring culture and global issues into every lesson!

コンからはがして下さい
51
1/1
ISBN：9784866930954
受注No：125360
受注日付：241211

コメント：3082
書店CD：187280
28

書店

日本が直面「する」
ミリタリーOR

小宮 享 Toru komiya